NAVAL, MAR
AND AIR FOl
UNIFORMS OF
WORLD WAR 2

A companion volume to *Army Uniforms of World War 2*,
written by Andrew Mollo and illustrated by
Malcolm McGregor

NAVAL, MARINE
and AIR FORCE
UNIFORMS of
WORLD WAR 2

ANDREW MOLLO

Illustrated by Malcolm McGregor

BLANDFORD PRESS
Poole   Dorset

Blandford Press Ltd
Link House, West Street,
Poole, Dorset BH15 1LL

First published 1975
© Blandford Press 1975

Set in 10/11 Garamond
Printed and bound by
Cox & Wyman Ltd, Fakenham, Norfolk

ISBN 0 7137 0725 9

CONTENTS

ACKNOWLEDGEMENTS

K. Barbarski; F. Bartholomé; K. C. Bastian; T. Brynhildsen of the Haermuseet Oslo; P. Buss, B.A. (Hons.); A. Campbell; W. Y. Carman, F.S.A., F.R. Hist. S.; Captain Cigala-Fulgosi, Royal Italian Navy Retd; R. M. Cook; B. L. Davis; Major A. Donald, Royal Marines, Retd; T. H. de Gebert; Dr. H. D. Langley, Division of Naval History, Smithsonian Institution, Washington D.C.; F. G. Longbon; J. Lorette, Musée Royal de l'Armée et d'Histoire Militaire, Brussels; J. Mollo; B. Mollo, National Army Museum, London; J. Munday, National Maritime Museum, Greenwich; Miss L. Mygh, Orlogsmuseet, Copenhagen; Group Captain K. M. Oliver, Commandant R.A.F. Catterick; F. Ollenschläger; Commander F. C. van Oosten, Royal Netherlands Navy, Retd; I. Fl. Rasmussen, Tøjhusmuseet, Copenhagen; G. Rosignoli; Major F. Silvo, Finnish Embassy, London; K. Stenman, Secretary of the Finnish Branch of the International Plastic Modellers Society; C. G. Sweeting, National Air and Space Museum, Smithsonian Institution, Washington D.C.; A. G. Szabo, and the people who for one reason or another wish to remain nameless. Also the staff of the photographic and exhibits departments and reference library of the Imperial War Museum, London, and in particular E. Hine, T. G. Charman, L. Milner, and M. J. Willis.

Without the continuous advice and assistance of Count E. G. Vitetti, Rome, Italy, this book would have been almost impossible to write.

To all the above our sincerest thanks.

Andrew Mollo
London 1975   *Malcolm McGregor*

PREFACE

This volume is the first postwar publication to describe and illustrate the naval and air force uniforms of the main combatant nations of World War 2. During the war, military and naval intelligence departments prepared manuals and posters to help their servicemen identify friend and foe alike, and since the war these rare publications have been the main source of information on the subject, and are now valuable collectors' items.

The great difficulty has been to strike a fair balance between regulation uniform, and what was actually worn by sailors and airmen in action. Many thousands of photographs – on which the present drawings are based – confirm that officers and men often wore precisely what they pleased, or found most practical for the tasks they had to perform. It has obviously not been possible to illustrate every item of uniform of every nation, nor describe every rank and trade badge; one could easily write a book of this length on each nation. Certain limits have had to be imposed. Firstly it has not been possible to include female auxiliaries, nor all the many uniformed, civil and para-military organisations which took an active part in the war. These organisations will probably be covered in a future volume. Illustrations and text have been designed to compliment each other and not overlap, so extensive references to illustrations in both this volume and in my previous work *Army Uniforms of World War 2* (hereafter referred to as A.U. followed by the page number and figure number) will be found in the text.

The description of cap badges, badges of rank, and rate, and trade and specialists' badges is not satisfactory, and so I have relied on the illustrations to show typical examples of some of these badges being worn.

Rank and rating badges have been broken down into groups for ease of description, but it must be remembered that a comparison between say a French *maître* and a British petty officer can only be approximate, since their responsibilities and authority were often very different.

A.M.

9

INTRODUCTION

Naval uniform as worn during World War 2, and even to this day, developed simultaneously in the major European navies during the last century. During this period the typical naval officer wore a blue frock coat and cocked hat, or so-called 'monkey jacket' or reefer and peaked cap, for informal everyday wear. Before World War 1 – and between the wars – the reefer became the basic service dress jacket, and the frock was limited to certain ceremonial or formal occasions until 1939. During the war the reefer was found to be impractical for many of the tasks that naval officers were called upon to perform and so, in its turn, it was reserved for special wear, while for everyday more practical types of utility clothing were introduced.

A uniform for seamen was not introduced in the British Royal Navy until 1857. Again one finds a remarkable similarity in the dress of sailors of one country and another, although closer inspection reveals a wealth of detailed differences. In some navies sailors wore their jumpers outside the trousers, while in others they tucked it inside; some shirts were plain and others striped; differences occurred in the scarf or 'silk' and in the way in which it was tied, in the blue jean collar, and in the lanyard. However the greatest variation will be found in the shape of the hat. While the British sailor wore a stiff hat with the crown only marginally wider than the band, most navies, particularly the Russian and German wore a cap with a wide crown. The cap ribbon or 'tally' was tied differently, and in some navies it hung down at the back of the head. During the war ribbons with names of ships, installations, and training establishments were replaced for security reasons by standard tallies such as 'H.M.S.' (His Majesty's Ship) or *Kriegsmarine* (War Fleet).

In most navies a distinction was drawn between officers and men in the seaman or executive branch, and those who performed civil duties such as administrators and doctors. In the British navy ratings in some branches wore traditional sailors' dress or 'square rig', while others wore 'fore and aft' rig with peaked cap and long jacket, but this degree of distinction was not common in other navies. Commissioned officers in the executive branch were known as 'executive' or 'military' officers. In many navies (and originally in the Royal Navy) only executive officers wore the loop or curl on the rank distinction lace on the cuffs and shoulder straps. In the German navy they were known as *Seeoffiziere* and wore a five-pointed star. In some navies only executive officers were known by naval titles, while those in other corps or branches used army ones. For example an admiral in a civil branch was known as a general.

The crews of warships have always been made up of craftsmen and specialists who were paid different rates of pay according to their capabilities, and so in the British Royal Navy all non-commissioned sailors were known as ratings. The badges which identified these trades and specialist roles are a highly complicated subject. Commander May in *Badges and Insignia of the British Armed Forces* devotes fifty pages to British badges alone, and since those of the other seafaring nations were almost as numerous, and their exact significance just as complicated, it would be impossible to scratch the surface of this subject internationally in one volume. Suffice it to say that a gun indicated that the rating was in the gunnery, and crossed flags in the visual signals branch. In most cases the devices indicated the branch. The addition of another device or star or bars indicated a higher-qualified rating. The combination of different devices such as crossed hammer and axe (international device for a smith) and torpedo showed that the rating was a torpedo artificer. By 1939 there was a remarkable similarity in the dress of naval personnel of all nationalities which the German uniform historian Herbert Knötel Jnr in his famous work *Handbuch der Uniformkunde* attributes to the British influence:

> Since 1860 the naval uniform of the seafaring nations was unusually standardised, and in the main the same items of clothing appeared in the same basic cut. The decisive factor in the development of these uniforms was Britain. Great Britain's fleet ruled the waves in the last century, and had then, and still has, a major influence on the whole appearance of naval uniform. The historical development in the twentieth century to the present day shows how naval uniform became more and more similar to the British pattern as regards cut and rank badges.

Knötel could hardly have foreseen the situation which arose after Germany's victories in 1940, when naval contingents from all over Europe sought shelter in British ports. Any national peculiarities in dress were soon eliminated, not so much out of desire, but because only British uniforms were available to replace national ones when they wore out. To increase efficiency rank badges and branch colours were sometimes standardised on the British practice, and many such alterations were retained after the war.

Surprisingly of the main combatants only Britain, the United States, the Netherlands and Italy had special marine formations with their own distinctive uniforms. Most other countries such as Germany, France, Japan and the Soviet Union had units of naval personnel trained to fight on land, but they wore naval uniforms.

Air forces originated in the flying services built up by the world's principal armies and navies before and during World War 1, or in the case of countries which gained their independence as a result of Allied victory, in the 1920's and 1930's. The British Royal Flying Corps and Royal Naval Air Service were amalgamated in 1918 and became the independent Royal Air Force. Many other air forces including two of the largest remained part of the army.

In 1918 a new light blue uniform was introduced for the R.A.F. but it was soon replaced by a more practical and popular grey-blue (hereafter referred to as grey) uniform which is still in use today. This was the forerunner of all air forces' uniforms, and was widely copied, before, and particularly after World War 2. It provided the model for the uniforms of the air forces of the Colonies and Dominions, except South Africa which retained army uniform, and Australia which adopted the cut and badges, but introduced a dark blue uniform. It was adopted by Germany in 1935, and by Greece, Belgium, Italy, Poland, Rumania and Yugoslavia. So faithfully did the Germans copy it that the same black mohair band appears on Luftwaffe caps. In one respect the R.A.F. was not copied and that was the introduction in August 1919 of special rank titles (Flight Lieutenant etc.) and badges of rank. Some countries adopted rank distinction lace on the cuffs – copied more from their navies than from anything else – but all retained army rank titles (General, Captain etc.)

Those air forces which retained army uniform or introduced army-type uniforms (Chinese, Hungarian etc.) almost universally adopted sky or light blue as their arm-of-service colour, the significance of which is of course obvious.

France called its air force the Air Army (and navy Sea Army), and introduced a naval-type dark blue uniform and rank badges. Although still in use in France, this style of uniform did not catch on abroad, except in Russia where it did not last very long.

NOMENCLATURE

As in the previous volume I have tried to standardise terms internationally in such a way as to make them immediately understandable to the reader, and eliminate the necessity of using two words when one will do.

Unless stated to the contrary blue refers to the dark blue-black or navy blue, and grey to the typical air force grey-blue when describing uniforms.

In order to differentiate between the traditional rectangular sailors' collar, and other kinds of uniform collar, I refer to the sailors' as the blue jean collar, after the material from which it was usually made. British ratings did not receive the short double-breasted peajacket, so I have used the current American term peacoat. Throughout I refer to lace as being flat and woven in metallic or fabric thread, as opposed to braid which is usually round or oval in section. In describing rank distinction lace which was usually worn on the cuffs and shoulder straps, I use 'ring' when it went right round (or was intended to go right round) the cuff, stripe if it was over 5 cm (2 in.) long, but not continuous, and bar if it was less than 5 cm long. Chevrons are described in their correct heraldic sense, with a chevron having its point uppermost, and an inverted chevron with its point downwards.

The division between one group of ratings or officers and another is not as straightforward as in the army, as the following notes will indicate:

Seamen | This group refers to all sailors in executive or civil branches. In the British Royal Navy they were known as boy, ordinary and leading seaman, with able seaman being limited to the seaman branch. In the majority of navies they were classified, e.g. seaman 1st class. In the German navy they were known by army ranks with prefix sailor e.g. *Matrosengefreiter*. In the French navy they were known as *matelots* and quartermasters. They were usually distinguished by a badge on the sleeve which was often combined with a branch (non-substantive) badge. In most navies the most junior rate did not wear a badge, while in others a branch badge on its own denoted a rate.

Petty officers | This group roughly corresponded to army senior non-commissioned officers, and petty officers often wore a peaked cap and tunic, whereas in the U.S. and Soviet navies they wore square rig. Rate badges usually consisted of chevrons. Chief petty officers were equivalent to more senior army non-commissioned officers and were entitled to wear officers' uniform, while in the French navy they wore rank distinction lace on the cap and cuffs like officers.

Warrant officers   In the British Royal Navy senior chief petty officers could be promoted to warrant and subsequently to commissioned warrant officers. In the French and Italian navies long-serving petty officers were elevated to the *Corps Officiers Mariniers* or *Corpo Reale Equipaggi Marittimi* respectively. They could then be promoted up to the rank of lieutenant, and were distinguished from regular officers by special rank badges.

Cadets
and Midshipmen   In the British Royal Navy cadets underwent training at the Royal Naval College, and then transferred to a ship for completion of their training as midshipmen. In the U.S. Navy they were called ensigns, and in others sub or junior lieutenants. In the Tsarist Russian navy they were called *Mishman* (Russified form of the British midshipman), but when this rank was reintroduced in the Soviet navy it signified a warrant officer.

In most navies officers were not divided into three groups as in the army, but into two – officers and flag officers, although there was usually a distinction in the rank badges for senior officers who corresponded to army field officers. For this reason I have described rank badges in three groups – lieutenants (equal to company officers), captains and commanders (equivalent to field officers) and flag officers (equivalent to general officers). In some navies such as the British where rank badges did not follow in an easily describable sequence, it has been necessary to describe each rank separately.

Lieutenants   This group covers the lowest three or four commissioned ranks, which sometimes includes ensigns and midshipmen or their equivalents.

Captains
and Commanders   This group usually consisted of two or three ranks.

Commodores   Intermediate group usually consisting of one rank, but

	two in the British Royal Navy, the senior of which, commodore 1st class, was almost indistinguishable from a rear admiral.
Flag officers	This group covers all officers with admirals' rank. In most navies there were three or four ranks, with admiral of the fleet or German *Grossadmiral* being roughly equivalent to an army field marshal. In some navies officers of flag rank in civil branches were known as generals.

The British Royal Air Force was unique in introducing special rank titles (e.g. squadron leader), while all other air forces retained army titles. To many it would seem rather strange to divide air force ranks into company, field and general officers, so instead I have used the following system:

Airmen	All ranks below non-commissioned officers.
N.C.O.s	Non-commissioned officers.
Warrant officers	Warrant officers which in some air forces were really senior n.c.o.s.
Junior officers	The first three or four commissioned ranks.
Senior officers	All officers from major to colonel inclusive.
General officers	Known in Britain as air officers this group corresponds to army general officers and usually comprised four ranks including the rank equivalent to field marshal. Also includes rank of air commodore in the R.A.F.

UNIFORM NOTES

BELGIUM Naval Corps

The *Corps de Marine* was formed during World War 1, and the uniform worn at the outbreak of war was the result of regulations issued on 26 January 1940.

Officers and petty officers (*maîtres*) wore a double-breasted blue jacket with two rows of five gilt metal buttons converging to the waist, side pockets with straight flaps, two small buttons at the back of the cuff on the outside, gold lace *passants*, and army pattern black cloth collar patches with light blue piping on the collar. It was worn with white shirt, black tie, matching long trousers, and black shoes and socks. Gloves were black or brown leather. The blue army pattern greatcoat had *passants* instead of shoulder straps. In bad weather any current commercial pattern of black or blue raincoat or cloak could be worn with uniform.

The peaked cap had a blue or white top, black band, black leather peak and gold chin cord. The cap badge was embroidered in gold and was surmounted by a circular enamel cockade in the national colours – red, yellow, and black. Priests had a plain black silk cap band, while line officers had gold or silver lace rings according to rank. Petty officers uniform was almost identical to officers, but had no *passants* or buttons at the cuff, and the rows of buttons on the front of the jacket were parallel. The peaked cap for chief petty officers (*premiers maîtres*) had a silver anchor surmounted by the national cockade on the front of the peaked cap, and silver chin cord, while all other ratings entitled to wear a peaked cap had a black leather chin strap.

Quartermasters and seamen wore the uniform illustrated in 1.

Rank was indicated as follows:

Quartermasters	Two diagonal scarlet lace stripes on the cuffs.
Petty officers (*maîtres*)	One to three diagonal gold lace stripes on the cuffs.
Chief petty officer	One six-pointed silver-embroidered star on the collar patches and one silver lace ring around the cap band.
Company officers	One to three six-pointed gold-embroidered stars on the collar patches, and one or two gold, or two gold with one silver lace ring between, on the cap band.

| Field officers | One to three six-pointed gold-embroidered stars with a gold stripe above on the collar patches, and four, or four gold with a silver between the second and third ring, or five gold lace rings on the cap band. |

From April 1941 Belgians serving in the *Section Belge* of the British Royal Navy wore British uniform with 'Belgium' shoulder flash, and sometimes the Belgian national colours on the left side of the hat or steel helmet. By 1955 three hundred and fifty six ratings and eighty officers were serving in the Royal Navy or in administrative posts.

BELGIUM   Royal Air Force

In 1929 an English-style grey uniform was introduced for flying personnel of the air force which formed part of the army. All non-flying personnel wore army uniforms [A.U. pp. 17–18].

The grey service dress for officers and regular senior n.c.o.s is illustrated in 2. N.C.O.s wore silver-embroidered or white metal badges. The side cap for officers was grey with black tassel in front and black piping for company, black lace for field, and gold lace around the sleeve of the cap for general officers. On the left front was worn a small white or gilt metal winged badge. The army pattern greatcoat was also made of grey cloth.

Pilots (3) wore a brown leather flying helmet, goggles, brown leather or khaki canvas overall with zip-fastener in front, and zip-fastenings on breast and leg pockets, and parachute.

Members of non-flying air force regiments wore army uniforms with light blue collar patches piped in red. Personnel of the Territorial Anti-Aircraft Guard wore on duty, a one-piece khaki overall with collar piped in red, and khaki side cap.

Rank badges were those of the Belgian army, except that general officers had gold-embroidered oak leaves on the cap band. General staff officers had a silver-embroidered *cartouche* on the collar patches.

Belgian personnel serving with the British Royal Air Force wore R.A.F. uniform with the 'Belgium' shoulder flash in light blue on a dark blue or grey ground.

The uniform of the Bulgarian navy closely resembled that of Tsarist Russia on which it was based.

The standard service dress for officers is shown in 5. The greatcoat was double-breasted with two rows of five gilt metal buttons, slanting side pockets with curved flaps, and half-belt at the back fastened with a button at each end. In hot weather officers wore a single-breasted white tunic with stand-collar and five gilt metal buttons, breast pockets with three-pointed Austrian-pattern flaps, and a white cap cover and matching long trousers with white canvas shoes, or long blue trousers with black leather shoes.

Chief petty officers wore the same basic uniform as officers. On the peaked cap they had a black leather chin strap.

Ratings wore a Russian-style bloused jumper with V-neck opening, gathered cuffs fastened with two brass buttons, and blue collar edged with white stripes. The shirt was striped in light blue and white. In winter they wore a short double-breasted peacoat with two rows of five brass buttons. The hat was worn with blue or white top, black rayon band with the name of the ship or installation i.e. 'Varna Base' in yellow or gold Cyrillic letters. Above the band on the front was worn an oval metal cockade in the national colours – white, green, and red.

All ranks wore their rank badges on the shoulder straps, and in addition line officers wore gold lace rings on the cuffs of the jacket. On the white summer jacket officers wore gold lace stripes on the outside of the cuffs.

Rank was indicated as follows:

Seamen	One gold lace stripe with blue line in the centre across the shoulder strap.
Petty officers	Two or three gold lace stripes with blue line in the centre across the shoulder straps which were edged with gold lace.
Chief petty officer	One wide gold lace stripe across the shoulder straps which were edged with gold lace.
Lieutenants	Gold-embroidered crown above one to three narrow gold lace rings on the cuffs, and gold lace shoulder straps with a blue stripe and none to three four-pointed white metal stars.

Captains and Commanders	Gold-embroidered crown above one to three narrow and one medium gold lace ring below, on the cuffs, and gold lace shoulder straps with two blue stripes and one to three four-pointed white metal stars.
Flag officers	Gold-embroidered crown above one to three narrow and one wide gold lace ring below, on the cuffs, and gold zigzag pattern lace shoulder straps with one to three four-pointed white metal stars.

BULGARIA   Royal Air Force

Although a grey uniform had been introduced before the war, many obsolete army khaki uniforms with closed-collar tunics were still being worn during the war.

The basic grey service dress for officers and senior n.c.o.s is illustrated in 4, but in addition officers could wear matching long trousers (generals with light blue *lampassen*). The greatcoat was double-breasted with dark grey fall collar piped in light blue, on which was worn scarlet collar patches piped in silver. In front it had two rows of silver buttons converging to the waist, turn-back cuffs piped in light blue, sloping side pockets with flap, and half-belt at the back fastened with a button at each end.

The side-cap was similar to the Italian pattern, and had a small version of the peaked cap badge on the front, and rank badges on the left side.

Other ranks wore a single-breasted tunic with closed stand-and-fall collar on which was worn light blue rectangular collar patches with a button at the top end, six buttons, pleated patch breast and side pockets all with Austrian-pattern flap and button, and pointed cuffs. Matching trousers were worn with black leather shoes or boots. The greatcoat was double-breasted, and fastened down the centre with one row of six buttons. The collar patches were as worn on the tunic, and the turn-back cuffs were piped in light blue. The slanting side pockets had a flap.

Equipment was brown leather, and the rectangular belt plate was made of brass.

Rank was indicated as follows:

Corporals	Plain light blue collar patches and light blue piped grey shoulder straps with one silver lace stripe with a blue line in the centre across the middle of the shoulder strap.

N.C.O.s	Plain light blue collar patches and light blue shoulder straps with two or three silver lace stripes with a blue line in the centre across the middle of the shoulder strap.
Warrant officer	Plain light blue collar patches and light blue shoulder straps with one wide silver lace stripe across the middle of the shoulder strap.
Potential officers	Light blue collar patches with one narrow and one medium wide silver grey horizontal bars, and light blue shoulder straps with one wide silver lace stripe across the middle and silver lace edging. One narrow silver lace bar on the side cap.
Junior officers	German army pattern collar patches in silver embroidery on light blue base, and silver lace shoulder straps with one light blue stripe and none to three four-pointed gilt metal stars. One narrow silver lace stripe on the side cap.
Senior officers	Collar patches as for company officers. Silver lace shoulder straps with two light blue stripes and one to three four-pointed gilt metal stars. One wide and one narrow silver lace stripes on the field cap.
General officers	Light blue collar patches embroidered with gold oak-leaves, and gold zigzag-pattern lace shoulder straps with one to three four-pointed white metal stars. One gold lace bar on the side cap.

CHINA   Navy

The newly established Republic of China introduced westernised naval uniform in 1913, which remained in use during the war, with the exception of various minor changes.

The basic service dress for officers is illustrated in 8. The white summer tunic was basically the same cut, but had five gilt metal buttons in front, and no lace trimming. It was worn with white sun helmet, matching long trousers, and white canvas shoes. The greatcoat was double-breasted with large fall-collar and two rows of five gilt metal buttons. There was a side pocket on the left hip only, and a matching hood which fastened under the chin with a tab and button.

The peaked cap was blue with black mohair band, black leather peak and gold-embroidered cap badge on the front.

Ratings wore a white shirt with blue taped neck opening, blue jumper with blue jean collar edged with two white stripes, black scarf, and white knife lanyard. The white jumper had in addition light blue cuffs. The English-pattern hat was blue with black silk ribbon with the name of the ship or installation in Chinese characters, and a gold anchor at each end. It was worn with blue or white top. There was also a straw hat with black pompom on the top, black tape binding around the brim, and black ribbon as on the hat. In winter ratings wore a short double-breasted peacoat with two rows of five black buttons, and turn-back cuffs. There was also a foul weather coat made of black oilskin with matching hood.

Rank was indicated by black (later gold) lace rings on the cuffs of the blue tunic, and by blue shoulder straps on the white tunic and blue greatcoat.

Seamen	One (seaman 3rd class) to three (1st class) red bars on the upper right sleeve. Engineering branch had one to three red chevrons.
Petty officers	Single or crossed red foul anchors on the upper right sleeve.
Lieutenants	Gold-embroidered open wheat wreath, or black lace circle above one medium, one narrow above one medium, or two medium gold or black lace rings on the cuffs. Three narrow gold lace stripes and one to three five-pointed white metal stars on the shoulder straps.
Captains and Commanders	Gold-embroidered open wheat wreath, or black lace circle above one narrow and two medium, or three or four medium gold or black lace rings on the cuffs. Two medium gold lace stripes and one to three five-pointed white metal stars on the shoulder straps. One row of gold-embroidery on the cap peak.
Commodores	Gold-embroidered open wheat wreath or black lace circle above one wide gold or black lace ring on the cuffs. Gold lace shoulder strap, and one row of gold embroidery on the cap peak.
Flag officers	Gold-embroidered open wheat wreath, or black lace circle above one wide, with one to three medium gold

or black lace rings above, on the cuffs. Gold lace shoulder straps with one to three five-pointed white metal stars, and gold-embroidered cap peak.

About 1943 the wheat wreath was replaced by the nationalist emblem, the 'white sun and blue sky', which was worn on the shoulder straps and above the rings on the cuffs. This emblem was also worn on the cap badge, except by the navy of the Japanese puppet state of Manuchukuo (Manchuria) which retained Chinese naval uniforms but replaced the nationalist emblem with the plum blossom.

Branch colours appeared on the shoulder straps as follows:

Branch	Colour
Ship constructors	Purple
Navigating officers	Light indigo blue
Ordnance	Pink
Wireless	Mauve
Surgeons	Scarlet
Judge Advocates	Grey
Bandmasters	Green
Paymasters	White

Members of the above branches did not wear the wheat wreath or lace ring above their rank rings, but naval aviators wore a winged bird above theirs.

CHINA   Air Force

The Air Force was established as an independent arm in the mid-1930's, and from the beginning it relied to a large extent on American machines, equipment, and training.

Air force personnel wore army uniforms [A.U. pp. 20–21 and 112]. The basic officer's service dress is shown in 9. Officers also wore a khaki peaked cap with light khaki band, and black leather peak and chin strap. The cap badge consisted of gold-embroidered wings with the enamel 'white sun and blue sky' badge in the centre. There was also a khaki side cap with brass winged propeller or 'white sun and blue sky' on the left front.

In the summer officers wore a white cap cover, and white cotton version of the khaki service dress. For everyday wear in hot weather officers had light khaki shirts and shorts.

Other ranks wore army uniforms, and ground crew various types of overalls. Towards the end of the war American clothing began to predominate.

Flying clothing (7) was mostly made in America under contract although captured Japanese clothing was extensively used.

Rank badges were worn on the cuffs until 1940 when they moved to the shoulder. At first badges were embroidered, but due to manufacturing difficulties they began to be made in metal and even plastic.

Other ranks	As army [A.U. p. 20].
Junior officers	Gold-embroidered or gilt metal blossom or winged bird above one to three gold-embroidered or gilt metal stripes on the cuffs and later on the shoulder straps.
Senior officers	Gold-embroidered or gilt metal blossom or winged bird above one wide with one to three medium gold-embroidered or gilt metal stripes above, on the cuffs and later on the shoulder straps.
General officers	Gold-embroidered or gilt metal blossom or winged bird above two wide and one to three narrow gold-embroidered or gilt metal stripes above, on the cuffs and later on the shoulder straps.

It is believed that only flying personnel wore the winged bird while all other non-flying officers wore the plum blossom. Pilots and observers also wore metal wings above the left breast pocket.

CROATIA   Navy

The Italian occupation authorities did not permit the formation of a Croatian navy, and so naval personnel served in the German navy in the so-called Naval Legion. The uniform was that of the German navy with a winged shield charged with the Croatian coat of arms on the cap and on the left breast in place of the German national emblem. They also wore a woven shield-shaped badge with the Croatian coat of arms ensigned by the label *Hrvatska* on the upper right sleeve. After the Italian capitulation a Croatian navy was formed, and new uniforms and insignia based on the German pattern were introduced.

The uniform for officers and petty officers consisted of a double-breasted blue jacket with two rows of four gilt metal buttons and slash side pockets with straight flaps. It was worn with white shirt, black tie, matching long trousers, and black leather shoes. The greatcoat was double-breasted.

The blue peaked cap had a black artificial mohair band, black peak, with one or two rows of gold-embroidered oak leaves according to senior rank, and black leather chin strap. The cap badge for officers was a foul anchor within an open oak wreath, while petty officers had an oval metal anchor badge.

For summer wear there was a single-breasted open white jacket with four gilt metal buttons and open patch breast and side pockets, and turn-back cuffs. It was worn with shoulder straps, white shirt, black tie, matching white trousers, and canvas shoes. The cap also had a white cover. There was a 'trenchcoat' in Raglan cut with matching cloth belt, and special rectangular rank badges for wear on the left front by officers. Petty officers wore their badges of rank on the upper left sleeve.

With certain orders of dress officers wore a brown leather waistbelt with brass buckle, and with undress uniform they wore the German pattern naval officers dagger, with a different pommel.

226 shows the basic dress for ratings. The inscription on the cap ribbon was *Ratna Mornarica*. The yellow metal oval cap badge had the letters N D H or *Nesavisna Država Hrvatska* (Independent State of Croatia) in the centre.

In addition to German-pattern shoulder straps for wear on the white tunic, greatcoat and raincoat, and gold lace rings for wear on the cuffs of the blue jacket, there was also a system of rank badges consisting of a rectangular blue cloth patch with the trefoil above short gold lace bars, in the same number and width as on the cuffs, for wear on foul weather and working clothes and on the trenchcoat by line officers only. Rank was indicated as follows:

Seamen	Anchor and one, two or three, or three red tape chevrons with a slide on the upper left sleeve. Blue cloth shoulder straps with one or two gilt metal trefoils. Mate or *Vodnik* had shoulder straps edged with gold lace.

N.C.O.s	Anchor and one, two or three horizontal gold lace bars underneath on the cuffs, and on the upper left sleeve of the 'trenchcoat'. Blue shoulder straps edged with gold lace on which were worn one to three gilt metal trefoils.
Midshipmen	One medium gold lace ring on the outside of the cuff only. Flat aluminium braid shoulder straps on dark blue base.
Lieutenants	Trefoil above one, two, or two medium with one narrow gold lace ring between on the cuffs. Flat aluminium braid shoulder straps with one to three gilt metal trefoils.
Captains	Trefoils above one to three medium above one wide gold lace ring on the cuffs. Flat interwoven aluminium braid shoulder straps on dark blue base with one to three gilt metal trefoils. One row of gold-embroidered oak leaves on the cap peak.
Flag officers	Trefoils within an open oak wreath above one medium, and one very wide gold lace ring on the cuffs. Two gold and one aluminium interwoven braid shoulder straps on cornflower blue base with one white metal trefoil. Two rows of gold-embroidered oakleaves on the cap peak.

CROATIA   Air Force

At first members of the Croatian Air Force wore the uniforms of the former Yugoslav Air Force but with rank badges on the collar. Members of the Croatian Air Force Legion which fought on the eastern front as part of the Luftwaffe wore German uniforms with a shield-shaped badge with the Croatian coat of arms ensigned by the legend *Hrvatska* in white, on the upper right sleeve. By May 1942 a new uniform was introduced which was almost identical to that of the German Luftwaffe. This uniform will only be described here in so far as it differed from the German pattern.

231 shows the basic officers service dress with side cap. The peaked cap was identical to the German pattern except that the cap badge was an aluminium-embroidered open oak wreath surmounted by a winged bird. The version for generals was embroidered in gold. Above this badge was worn an oval white metal badge with the letters NDH in the centre. (*Continued on page 109.*)

THE COLOUR PLATES

1. Petty officer

2. Air Force officer

3. Fighter pilot

4. Air Force officer

6. Seaman

5. Naval officer

7. Fighter pilot

9. Air Force officer

8. Admiral

10. Seaman

11. Naval officer

12. Air Force officer

13. Seaman

15. Air Force officer

14. Fighter pilot

16. Petty officer

18. Chief petty officer

17. Naval officer

19. Seaman

20. Seaman

21. Petty officer

22. Marine

23. Marine officer

24. Marine officer

25. Air Force General

26. Air Force officer

27. Bomber pilot

French Air Force 1943—45

28. Air Force officer

29. Air Force officer

30. Airman

31. Polish Air Force officer

33. Czech Air Force sergeant

32. Czech Air Force sergeant

German Navy 1939—45

34. Seaman

35. Admiral

36. Seaman

37. Petty officer

38. Naval officer

39. Seaman

40. Seaman

41. Naval officer

42. Seaman

43. Naval officer

44. Seaman

45. Admiral

46. Coastal policeman

48. Naval Hitler Youth

47. Transport Fleet Speer petty officer

49. Officer

50. General

51. Officer

52. Fighter pilot

54. Bomber pilot

53. Reich Marshal

55. Fighter pilot

57. Fighter pilot

56. Fighter pilot

58. Corporal

59. General

60. Fighter pilot

61. Russian officer

62. Spanish officer

63. Belgian NSKK man

64. Corporal

65. General

66. Parachutist

67. Grenadier

68. General

69. Sergeant

70. Anti-Aircraft helper

71. A.R.P. officer

72. Air Police officer

73. Australian seaman

74. Admiral

75. Petty officer

76. New Zealand officer

78. Leading seaman

77. Naval officer

79. Leading seaman

80. Coxswain

81. Visual signaller

British Royal Navy 1939—45

82. Naval officer

83. Naval officer

84. Seaman

85. Able seaman

86. Naval officer

87. Leading seaman

88. Air gunner

90. Cadet rating

89. Naval officer

91. Bugler

92. Officer

93. Marine

94. South African seaman

95. Cingalese seaman

96. Indian seaman

97. Flight sergeant

98. Air Marshal

99. Air Force officer

100. Air Force officer

101. Air Force officer

102. Airman

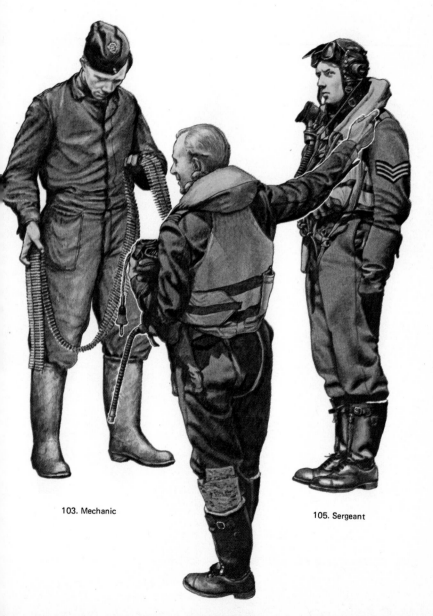

103. Mechanic

105. Sergeant

104. Fighter pilot

106. New Zealand pilot

107. Pilot

108. Pilot

109. Iraqi sergeant

111. Leading aircraftsman

110. Leading aircraftsman

112. Observer

113. Airman

114. Cadet

115. Australian pilot

117. South African pilot

116. New Zealand pilot

Foreign Colonial and Dominion personnel serving with the R. A. F. 1940—45

118. Canadian officer

120. West African aircrew cadet

119. American officer

121. Norwegian officer

123. French sergeant

122. Polish officer

124. Admiral

126. Corporal

125. Petty officer

127. Air Force officer

128. Admiral

129. Corporal

130. Seaman

131. Admiral

132. Officer

133. Seaman

135. Officer

134. Admiral

136. Marine

137. Officer

138. Marine

139. Officer

141. Fighter pilot

140. General

142. Fighter pilot

144. Officer

143. Marshal

145. Corporal

146. Officer

147. Padre

Royal and Republican Italian Parachute Troops 1941—45

148. Parachutist

149. Officer

150. Sergeant

151. Petty officer

152. Officer

153. Seaman

154. Officer

155. Admiral

156. Petty officer

157. Petty officer

158. Officer

159. Petty officer

160. Cadet

162. Airman

161. Suicide pilot

163. Seaman

165. Air Force officer

164. Naval officer

166. Marine

167. Marine sergeant

168. Marine sergeant

169. Airman

170. Air Force officer

171. Petty officer

Polish Navy 1939—45

172. Seaman

173. Officer

174. Seaman

175. Officer

176. Officer

177. Sergeant

178. Rumanian fighter pilot

180. Slovak Air Force officer

179. Rumanian admiral

181. Midshipman

182. Naval officer

183. Naval officer

184. Petty officer

185. Shore patrolman

186. Chief petty officer

187. Admiral

188. Admiral

189. Seaman

190. Petty officer

192. Seaman

191. Seaman

193. Pilot

194. Officer

195. Officer

196. Corporal

198. Officer

197. Marine

199. Marine

200. Samoan Fita-Fita

201. Officer

202. Officer

204. Military policeman

203. General

205 Aircrew

206. Officer

207. Groundcrew

208. Aircrew

209. Aircrew

210. Aircrew

211. Officer

212. Officer

213. Petty officer

214. Seaman

215. Officer

216. Seaman

217. Leading seaman

218. Admiral

219. Seaman

220. Officer

221. Sergeant

222. Officer

223. Officer

225. Aircrew

224. Parachute officer

226. Croatian seaman

228. Croatian officer

227. Yugoslav officer

229. Yugoslav officer

230. Yugoslav officer

231. Croatian officer

Naval Officers Swords

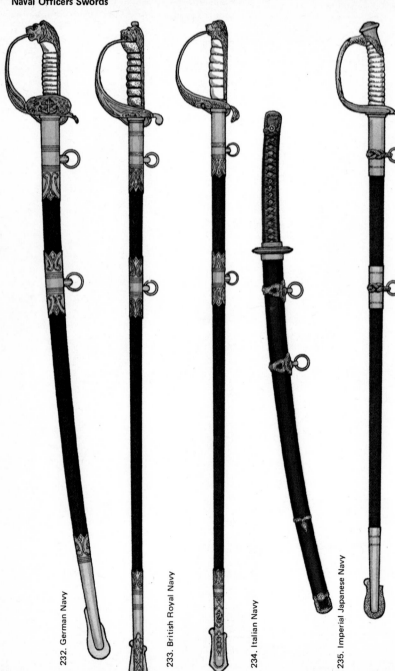

232. German Navy

233. British Royal Navy

234. Italian Navy

235. Imperial Japanese Navy

236. United States Navy

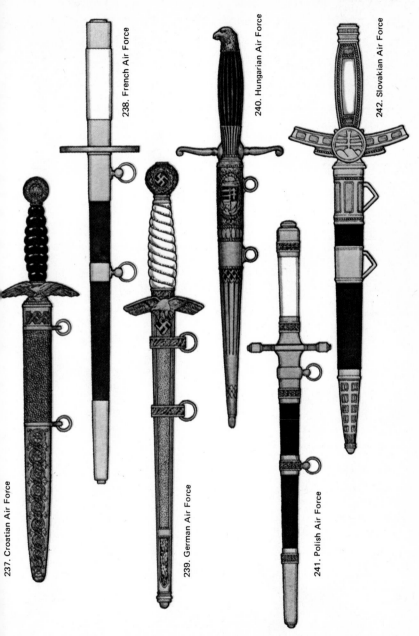

Air Force Officers Daggers

237. Croatian Air Force

238. French Air Force

239. German Air Force

240. Hungarian Air Force

241. Polish Air Force

242. Slovakian Air Force

Seamens collars and hat ribbons

243. Croatian Navy

244. German Navy

245. Royal Italian and Republican Navies

246. Imperial Japanese Navy

247. United States Navy

248. Soviet Russian Navy

Rank badges were identical to the German pattern but included the additional rank of junior lieutenant or midshipman.

Airmen	None to two white-metal wings on the collar patches and none to two white-metal trefoils on the shoulder straps.
N.C.O.s	Aluminium lace on the tunic and greatcoat collar patches and on the shoulder straps, and one to three white metal wings on the collar patches, and one to three white-metal trefoils on the shoulder straps.
Junior officers	Collar patches edged with twisted aluminium cord, and embroidered with aluminium wire oak leaves and none to three wings. Flat aluminium braid shoulder straps one to two wings within. Three interwoven aluminium chin cords on the peaked cap.
Senior officers	Collar patches edged with twisted aluminium cord, and embroidered with aluminium wire open oak wreath with one to two wings within. Three interwoven aluminium braids on the shoulder strap and one to three gilt-metal trefoils. Wide interwoven aluminium chin cords on the peaked cap.
Generals	Scarlet collar patches edged in twisted gold cord, and gold-embroidered open oak wreath with one to three gold-embroidered wings within. Two gold and one aluminium interwoven braid shoulder straps on scarlet base with one to three white-metal trefoils.
Marshal	Collar patches as for generals but with Croatian coat of arms ensigned by wings in the centre. Shoulder straps as for generals but with crossed batons in white metal.

Branch colours appeared as collar patches, and as piping on other ranks, and as base of officers shoulder straps as follows:

Branch	Colour
Generals	Scarlet
Flying personnel	Light blue
Anti-Aircraft artillery	Scarlet
Technical services	Brown
Supply	Green
Auxiliary units	Grey

CZECHOSLOVAKIA Air Force

After the German annexation Czech air force personnel made their way to France where they served as part of the French air force. They wore French uniform with Czech cap badge, badges of rank, and pilot's and observer's badges (32).

After the defeat of France, Czech personnel went to England in July 1940 where an independent Czech air force was formed. Personnel received R.A.F. uniform with 'Czechoslovakia' shoulder flash, while pilots, observers, and air gunners continued to wear their former qualification badges.

DENMARK Royal Navy

World War 2 naval uniform dated from the 1870's, and was very similar to that worn by the Royal Navy.

Officers, chief petty officers, and petty officers wore an open double-breasted blue jacket with two rows of four gilt metal buttons, side pockets were straight with flap, and it was worn with white shirt, black tie, matching long trousers and black leather shoes. The greatcoat was double-breasted with two rows of six gilt metal buttons, slanting side pockets with straight flap, and half-belt fastened at each end with a button. Gold lace rings were also worn on the cuffs of the greatcoat.

The peaked cap was blue with black mohair band, and black leather peak and chin strap. In the summer months it was worn with a white cover. The cap badge was basically the oval cockade in the Danish colours – red, and white, with a gilt metal foul anchor in the centre and gold-embroidered oak wreath which began with two leaves for petty officers, four for chief petty officers, six for lieutenants, captains and commanders, and twelve for flag officers.

10 shows the basic rating's uniform. The inscription on the cap ribbon was *KGL. Marine.*

In hot weather officers wore a white cap cover or sun helmet, single-breasted white tunic with stand collar and five gilt metal buttons in front, breast pockets with pointed flap, and two small buttons at the back of the cuff on the outside, long white trousers, and white canvas shoes. The white uniform for ratings consisted of a white hat cover, white jumper with blue collar and black scarf, and the cuffs fastened with a single brass button; shoes were black leather.

Rank was indicated by gold lace rings on the jacket and greatcoat cuffs, and on blue shoulder straps on the white tunic. Each rank group had its own cap badge – the higher the rank group the fuller the gold-embroidered wreath.

Leading seaman	Crossed red branch badge on upper sleeves.
Petty officers (*Underkvartermestre*)	Two or three yellow tape chevrons on the upper sleeves.
Chief petty officers (*Kvartermestre*)	One to three 9 cm (3·5 in.) long gold lace stripes on the cuffs.
Midshipmen (*Kadetter*)	One gold lace ring, Class A cadets one gold lace ring with a curl on the cuffs and shoulder straps.
Lieutenants	One narrow, one narrow above one very narrow, or two narrow gold lace rings with a curl on the only or uppermost on the cuffs and shoulder straps.
Captains and Commanders	Two narrow with one very narrow between, three narrow, two narrow with two very narrow between or four narrow gold lace rings with a curl on the uppermost, on the cuffs and shoulder straps.
Flag officers	One wide gold lace ring with one narrow above and two below, two wide gold lace rings with one narrow above and one below, and three wide gold lace rings with one narrow above with a curl on the uppermost on the cuffs and shoulder straps.

The various corps or branches were identified as follows:

Branch	Badge
Reserve	R superimposed on anchor inside curl.
Aviation	F inside curl.
Coastal artillery	K inside curl.
Engineers	Crimson backing to rings and crossed anchor and propeller in gold in place of the curl.
Intendence	White backing to rings and crossed anchor and rod of Mercury in gold in place of the curl.
Medical	Scarlet backing to rings and crossed Aesculapius and anchor in place of the curl.

DENMARK   Army Air Force

The air force came into being in the 1920's as part of the army, with its
personnel wearing army uniforms, and officers that of their former unit,
and army badges of rank.

Officers wore the M.1923 khaki service dress with either open (12) or
closed-collared tunic. Gold-embroidered wings for pilots and observers
were worn on the right breast.

Flying clothing and equipment of British manufacture was used by
both the army and naval air services.

Following the German invasion some air force personnel escaped to
England, where they served with the R.A.F. or in Norwegian units in
England. The shoulder flash 'Denmark' however was not officially
introduced until 1944.

Another group of Danes escaped to Sweden where they formed an air
force group as part of the Danish Brigade, and wore Swedish flying
clothing and equipment.

FINLAND   Navy

The navy came into existence after World War 1, during the country's
struggle for independence. Naval dress followed closely the British
pattern.

Officers and chief petty officers wore an open double-breasted blue
jacket with two rows of four or five buttons, open left breast pocket, and
side pockets with straight flaps. It was worn with white shirt, black tie,
matching long trousers and black shoes. The greatcoat was double-
breasted.

In addition to the dark blue peaked cap with blue or white top, and
gold-embroidered cap badge, there was a blue side cap with light blue
piping, black leather chin strap, and circular cockade in the national
colours.

The basic dress for ratings is illustrated in 13. There was also a fleece-
lined beige foul weather suit with attached hood, patch breast and side
pockets with flap, tab and button on the cuffs and matching trousers.
Members of the Coastal artillery still wore the obsolete grey M.1922
uniform with dark grey cuffs and collar.

Rank was indicated as follows:

Leading seamen	One yellow lace chevron on the upper left sleeve.
Petty officers	Two to four gold lace chevrons on the upper left sleeve.
Warrant officers	One wide gold lace chevron on the upper left sleeve.
Lieutenants	Gold-embroidered lion above one, two, or two medium with one narrow gold lace ring between, on the cuffs and shoulder.
Commanders and Commodores	Gold embroidered lion above three medium and one narrow, or four medium gold lace rings on the cuffs and shoulder straps, and one row of gold-embroidered oak leaves on the cap peak.
Flag officers	Gold-embroidered lion above one to three medium with one wide gold lace ring beneath, on the cuffs and shoulder straps, and two rows of gold oakleaves on the cap peak.

Reserve officers had zigzag lace rings.

The following corps were distinguished by coloured backing to the cuff rings as follows:

Corps	Colour
Engineering	Purple
Paymasters	As line but lion and rings in silver.
Surgeons	Scarlet
Supply	Six-pointed star in place of lion; star and rings in silver.

Ratings wore red branch badges, and petty officers gold, both above their chevrons.

Personnel serving in motor torpedo boats wore a gilt metal badge on the left breast.

FINLAND   Air Force

The Air Force began to be formed in 1918 as part of the army, and by the outbreak of war consisted of three flying regiments and an independent squadron.

The blue service dress for officers and regular senior non-commissioned officers is illustrated in 15. The greatcoat was double-breasted with two rows of four gilt metal buttons converging to the waist, cloth belt with metal buckle, and sloping side pockets with flap.

Additional head-dress included a blue side cap, and a winter version of the same which was made from black lamb's wool. On the front was worn a circular cockade in the national colours above a circular red cockade bearing the Finnish lion in gilt metal.

During the war those pilots who possessed the blue uniform continued to wear it on special occasions, or combined with items of army grey clothing, when on active service.

Rank was indicated as follows:

Corporals	One yellow chevron on the collar patches.
N.C.O.s	Two to four yellow lace chevrons on the collar patches on army pattern uniform, or on the upper left sleeve of the blue uniform.
	Sergeant-major one wide yellow chevron on the collar patches, and one wide gold lace chevron on the upper left sleeve.
Junior officers	One to three small gilt metal rosettes on the blue collar patches which were edged with one black line, on the army uniform, and one, two, or two narrow with one very narrow gold lace stripe between, on the cuffs of the blue uniform.
Senior officers	One to three large gilt metal rosettes on the blue collar patches which were edged with two black lines, on the army uniform, and one to three narrow with one wide gold lace stripe above, on the cuffs of the blue uniform.
General officers	One to three gilt metal lions on the blue collar patches which were edged with one wide and one narrow black-embroidered lines, on the army uniform, and one to three narrow above one very wide gold lace stripe, on the cuffs of the blue uniform.

FRANCE

Naval uniform as worn during World War 2 was the result of alterations made to existing regulations for officers in 1931, and petty officers in 1922. Ratings dress dates from 1858.

Officers service dress is shown in 17, and petty officers in 18. Not shown are the two small buttons at the back of the cuff, the gold-embroidery on the collar, and rectangular patch in the corps colour with three buttons, which was worn by generals (officers with flag rank but not serving in the line). The blue jacket could also be worn with white cap cover and white linen trousers and canvas shoes. The white tunic was open and single-breasted with four buttons in front, and breast and side pockets with straight flaps. There was also a light khaki drill uniform for wear in hot weather.

The greatcoat was double-breasted with two rows of five buttons, gold-embroidered *passants*, side pockets with straight flaps, half-belt at the back fastened with four buttons. There was also a double-breasted blue raincoat in civilian cut without insignia.

The peaked cap was blue with black leather peak and chin strap. Flag officers had gold chin cords and various patterns of gold-embroidery according to corps on the cap band. On the front line officers and flag officers had a gold embroidered open laurel wreath with a foul anchor in the centre while generals and officers serving in other corps had a different badge in the centre. Flag officers also had a 'sailing' cap without gold-embroidery around the band, and with an oval blue cloth cap badge edged in gold on which was affixed five-pointed silver stars according to rank.

Petty officers could wear the same uniform as officers when walking-out and for certain other special occasions, but normally they wore the uniform illustrated in 18. The greatcoat was also the same as the officer's pattern, but the walking-out raincoat was the same as that issued to other ratings.

The various types of dress worn by ratings are illustrated in 19, 20, and 21, but in addition there were a number of other items of working and foul-weather clothing. Mechanics and firemen wore a bright blue one-piece overall and side cap with a red anchor on the left side. Foul-weather clothing was made of black or yellow oilskin. Crews of motor torpedo boats and other fast craft received a special outfit consisting of cloth helmet, special lined waterproof jacket with 'plastron' front and two rows of four buttons, and sea boots with wooden soles. For very cold weather there was a cloth 'Canadian' coat lined with sheepskin, grey woollen scarf and sea boots.

In very hot weather officers and ratings wore a white sun helmet with metal version of the cap badge for officers and petty officers, and yellow metal anchor on the front for other ratings, who also wore the cap ribbon. In 1925 a new tropical dress (16) was introduced which consisted of a short-sleeve white cotton shirt with square neck opening. The neck opening and sleeves were edged with two dark blue lines. On the left breast ratings wore a blue anchor within a rectangular blue striped border. Underneath the anchor were worn one to three blue stripes according to rank. The shirt was worn with matching long trousers, white cap cover or helmet, and white canvas shoes.

Rank was indicated as follows:

Seamen and Quartermasters	One wide or two to three diagonal red lace stripes on the cuffs. Provisional leading seamen diagonal red lace stripe on upper left sleeve. One to three horizontal blue stripes on the left breast of the special summer uniform.
Petty officers (*Maîtres*)	One wide, or after two years service two or three narrow diagonal gold lace stripes on the cuffs, and gold lace chevrons on the shoulder straps.
Warrant officers (*Officiers mariniers*)	One medium gold and one narrow silver, one medium gold and one narrow gold lace ring with a narrow silver ring between and a rectangular vertical blue cloth patch with three buttons transversing them on the cuffs. Same number colour and width of lace on the shoulder straps with a blue cloth patch with two buttons crossing them. One medium gold lace ring around the cap band.
Midshipmen (*Aspirants*)	One medium gold lace ring broken with dark blue squares on the cuffs and shoulder straps.
Ensigns and Lieutenants	One to three medium gold lace rings on the cuffs, shoulder straps, and around the cap band.
Captains	Four medium gold, three medium gold with two silver between, or five medium gold lace rings on

	the cuffs, shoulder straps, and around the cap band.
Flag officers	Two to five five-pointed silver stars on the cuffs, shoulder straps which were edged in gold, and on the front of the cap band, which was also embroidered with oak leaves.

Branch colours appeared as a small rectangular patch at the back of the cuff of generals, and as backing to the rank distinction lace on the cuffs and shoulder straps of officers. Warrant officers had a rectangular patch bearing three buttons on the outside of the cuff.

Corps	Colour
Line, equipage, and administration	Uniform cloth.
Directors of music	Azur blue velvet.
Mechanical engineers	Violet velvet.
Reserve	Bright blue velvet.
Engineers and naval artillery	Black velvet.
Commissariat	Brown velvet (silver lace rings).
Medical	Crimson velvet.
Chemists and pharmacists	Bright green velvet.
Hydrographical professors	Pale violet velvet.
Recruiting and administrative staff of naval establishments	Ash grey velvet.
Interpreters and naval cypher officers	Blue velvet.
Dental surgeons	Dark grey velvet.

Specialist badges were, with few exceptions, worn on the upper left sleeve, and on the greatcoat and peacoat collar.

Naval aviators wore a circular white metal badge consisting of a foul anchor within a rope circle on which was applied the following gilt metal devices:

Branch	Badge
Pilots	Wings ensigned by five-pointed star.
Flying mechanics, radio telegraphists, gunners, and observers	Five-pointed star and one wing.
Balloon pilots	Wings ensigned by cogwheel.
Aerodrome observers	Cogwheel and one wing.

In July 1940 the Free French Navy (*Forces Navales France Libre*) was officially formed in Britain, while other small units were also established in other Free French territories and colonies.

Personnel continued to wear French naval uniform with the addition, from July 1940, of the Cross of Lorraine in enamelled metal or cloth for officers (17), and cloth for ratings, which was worn on the right breast. A new cap ribbon with the letters F.N.F.L. or the complete legend in yellow rayon or gold wire letters replaced the existing pattern.

Fusiliers Marins

Naval disembarkation companies, and naval personnel serving on land as well as naval infantry (*Fusiliers Marins*) wore standard naval dress but were also issued with a blue greatcoat, infantry pattern steel helmet, white or grey canvas leggings, and infantry equipment and arms. Amongst the many marine units which were formed during the war in the Middle East, were three battalions of *Fusiliers Marins*. The first of these was expanded into an Armoured Reconnaissance Regiment, and fought in Italy and France as part of the famous 2nd French (Leclerc) Armoured Division.

Most French marines trained and equipped by the British wore light khaki drill or battle dress, while retaining their French naval head-dress (22).

The Reconnaissance Regiment was equipped by America, and its personnel wore U.S. army combat clothing, with their naval head-dress, and yellow anchor painted on the front of the American steel helmet.

FRANCE   Air Army and Free French Air Forces

Air force uniform was regularised in July 1934, and being basically in dark or *Louise* blue it bore a marked similarity to the uniform of the French navy. After the German invasion air force personnel were equipped and trained by Great Britain and the United States of America, whose uniforms they also wore, so that the French uniform was worn almost exclusively as a walking-out dress by those who possessed it.

The basic service dress for officers and n.c.o.s is illustrated in 26. The greatcoat was double-breasted with fall collar, and two rows of six gilt metal buttons, slanting side pockets with flaps, turn back-cuffs, half-belt at the back fastened with two buttons, and gold-embroidered *passants* on the shoulders.

The peaked cap was blue with black band (woven silk on the working or everyday cap) on which generals had one or two rows of gold-embroidered oak leaves according to rank. The chin strap was made of two narrow gold cords. On the front of the cap above the band was worn a pair of gold-embroidered wings with the number of the formation for officers, gold star for staff officers, or silver stars for generals. Members of the colonial air force had the anchor.

With full dress officers wore a dagger (238) suspended from two blue leather straps. The knot (*dragonne*) was in matt gold for general officers and gold interwoven with blue silk for other officers. The tassels were in gold for all ranks.

Senior n.c.o.s wore the same basic uniform as officers except that the tunic had a matching cloth belt, five buttons in front, and the breast pockets had pleats. Other ranks wore a black beret, or peaked cap with black leather peak and chin strap, and orange piping and winged badge in front. The single-breasted tunic or *vareuse* was made of a coarser and lighter blue material, and was single-breasted with six brass buttons, side pockets with flap, fall collar, and was worn with matching long trousers, blue shirt, black tie, and black shoes or ankle boots. The obsolete horizon-blue infantry pattern greatcoat was in the process of being replaced by a blue version of the cavalry pattern greatcoat in 1937.

Aerodrome troops (*Base d'Aérostation*) in field service dress wore the armoured troop pattern steel helmet [A.U. 211], with stamped winged badge on the front, and infantry pattern brown leather equipment. In the tropics or on duty in France during the summer, all ranks wore a khaki drill uniform in the same basic cut as the blue uniform. In the tropics a white or light khaki sun helmet was also worn.

Rank was indicated as follows:

Airmen	One or two orange lace chevrons on the cuffs, and one vertical orange stripe on the front of the cap band. *Caporal-chef* two orange lace chevrons on the cuffs, and one diagonal gold lace stripe on the upper sleeves. Gold chin strap and gold piping around the top of the cap band.
N.C.O.s	One to three gold lace chevrons on the cuffs, and gold lace chin strap and gold piping around the top

of the cap band. *Adjudants* one silver, and *Adjudants Chefs* one gold lace ring with red stripe in the centre around the cuffs and cap band, and gold chin cords.

Junior officers — One to three gold lace rings around the cuffs and cap band.

Senior officers — Four gold, three gold with two silver rings between, and five gold lace rings around the cuffs and cap band.

Generals — Two to five five-pointed gold stars on the cuffs and cap badge. *Général de Brigade* one row of gold-embroidered oak leaves around the cap band with row of gold braid above. *Général de Division* two rows of gold oak leaves and one gold braid above. General commanding a region, and general who was a member of the Supreme War Council two rows of oak leaves, and one or two rows of silver braid respectively.

On the everyday or working cap the lace stripes were embroidered on a padded blue cloth oval, and on the greatcoat the rings were only 35 mm (1·3 in.) long.

Branch colours and formation numbers in orange appeared on other ranks blue collar patches as follows:

Branch	*Piping*
Light defence (fighter) squadrons	Green
Mixed squadrons	Yellow
Reconnaissance and observer squadrons	Blue
Heavy defence (bomber) squadrons	Red
Aerodromes, air bases and units administered by Air Companies	Mauve
Meteorological company	White
Air battalions and the administrative companies of these battalions	Grey

Non-commissioned flying personnel and specialists wore the following badges on their collar patches:

Pilot and Observer	Winged star.
Gunner, Mechanic and Radio operator	Winged grenade.

Non-flying specialist	Cogwheel
Meteorologists	Grenade
North African formations	Corps or group number above a half moon.
Colonial air force	Foul anchor.

Pilots and other qualified (*breveté*) flying personnel wore a circular white metal oak wreath with the following badges in gilt metal applied:

Pilots	Gilt wings ensigned by five-pointed star. By tradition usually worn at 45 degrees angle.
Balloon pilots	As for pilots but star replaced by cogwheel.
Cadet pilot and observer	Winged five-pointed star.
Cadet balloon pilot, mechanic and observer	Winged cogwheel.

After the defeat of France, a number of French air force units were scattered over the Middle East, Africa, and even Haiti, and had to be re-grouped, trained and equipped first by Britain and then America.

Members of the *Forces Aériennes Françaises Libres* serving alongside the R.A.F. continued to wear French uniform, or blue battledress (123). From January 1943 America undertook to provide uniforms and flying clothing for the rapidly expanding F.A.F.L.

In November 1943, the 3rd French Fighter Group arrived in Russia, and having been equipped with Soviet aircraft, fought with the 1st Soviet Air Army on the eastern front. Having participated in the forcing of the river Nieman in Lithuania, the regiment became known as *Normandie-Nieman*. Its personnel wore French air force uniform (29) with 'Normandy' in white Cyrillic letters on the right, and in Latin letters on the left sleeve at shoulder height.

White Cyrillic letters on the right sleeve at shoulder height.

On French blue, and American khaki service dress, rank badges were to be worn on blue cloth patches on the cuffs. On all other types of French, British, or American working uniforms, rank badges were to be worn either on a blue cloth slide on the shoulder straps, or on a blue cloth tab on the front of coats and jackets without shoulder straps. During the war officer's rank badges remained virtually unaltered, except that the lace rings instead of going right round the cuff, were only 5 cm (2 in.) long. Other ranks wore the following:

Soldier 1st class	One red lace chevron or diagonal stripe on the cuffs, or on the front of working dress.
Corporals	Two to three red lace chevrons or diagonal stripes on the cuffs or front of working dress.
Sergeants	One to three gold lace chevrons or diagonal stripes on the cuffs. Sergeant-Major three gold lace stripes or chevrons with one horizontal gold lace stripe beneath.
Adjudants (Warrant officers)	One silver or gold lace stripe with a red line in the centre, on the cuffs, shoulder straps, and left front of the side cap.
Aspirants	Knot in gold lace with red line in the centre on both cuffs or on the shoulder straps.

A new system of indicating the branch, by the colour of the cloth ground of the cap badge, and the colour of the edging of the rank lace was introduced:

Corps	*Colour*	*Cap badge colour*
Flying personnel	Blue cloth	Gold
Mechanical corps	Purple velvet	Gold
Administrative corps	Brown cloth	Gold
Medical corps	Maroon velvet	Silver
Gendarmerie	Blue cloth	Silver

GERMANY   War Navy

Naval uniform as worn during World War 2, was a development of that introduced in the Prussian navy in 1848.

The basic service dress for officers is illustrated in 35, and it was also worn by cadets, petty officers, who had two rows of five buttons, and administrative officials with officers rank, who wore white metal buttons and badges. With certain orders of dress the jacket could be worn with matching breeches and boots. The greatcoat was double-breasted with two rows of six gilt or silver buttons, slanting side pockets with rounded flap, and turn-back cuffs. The half-belt fastened in the centre with one button, and the false pocket flaps each had three buttons. Flag officers had cornflower blue lapels. The peaked cap was blue with black mohair band, black leather peak and chin strap for petty officers, and blue cloth covered peak with gold-embroidery according to commissioned rank. The national emblem and oak wreath were embroidered in gold wire or yellow silk, or made in yellow metal for petty officers. Administrative officials wore silver cap badges, and those with officers rank wore silver chin cords, and flag officers gold ones.

Ratings uniforms are illustrated in 36. In the summer months, or when serving in the tropics ratings wore a white jumper with blue jean collar and pointed cuffs. All insignia on the white jumper was in cornflower blue, except the specialist training badges which were in red. In addition to the regulation pre-war summer uniforms, personnel serving in the tropics could wear the M.40 khaki drill sun helmet with detachable white cotton cover. At first a large yellow metal national emblem was worn on the front, but this was later changed to the same metal shields as worn on the army sun helmet. The rank group of the wearer was indicated by the number and thickness of gold braids worn around the base of the headpiece. Officers also often wore a short-sleeved white Aertex tennis shirt without rank badges. Typical tropical working rig for ratings consisted of the white 'boarding' or side cap, white sports vest with large cornflower blue national emblem on the chest, white working trousers, and brown canvas shoes. In 1943 the khaki brown tropical uniform illustrated in 37 was introduced. Additional items were an open single-breasted tunic with four light khaki-painted anchor buttons, pleated patch breast and side pockets with three-pointed flap and button, and round cuffs, and matching long or short trousers and breeches.

In addition to the many items of working and foul-weather clothing introduced during the war, some of which are illustrated in 40-42, there was also a grey-brown denim 'battle-dress' type uniform, and it has been suggested that the first issue was in fact made from stocks of captured British clothing, but that thereafter it was manufactured in Germany. The blouse was single-breasted with stand-and-fall collar pleated patch breast pockets with pointed flap and button, matching shoulder straps, waistband fastened on the right hip with flat metal slide buckle, and sleeves gathered into a cuff which was fastened with one small button. All exposed buttons were attached by rings, and were the normal German naval pattern. Petty officers wore gold or yellow lace on the front and bottom edge of the collar points (not all round), and sometimes these 'angles' were cut from metal.

Officers and officials with officer rank wore their rank badges on the cuffs of the blue jacket, and on army pattern shoulder straps on all other types of uniform. Chief petty officers wore their rank badges on the shoulder straps of all uniforms. Other ratings wore their badges on the upper left sleeve. The colour of the lace and chevrons worn by ratings varied according to the colour of the uniform on which they were worn.

Uniform	*Chevrons/lace*
Blue and field-grey	Gold or yellow.
White	Cornflower blue.
Khaki brown	Cornflower blue or yellow.

Rank was indicated as follows:

Seamen (*Matrosen*)	One to three inverted chevrons on the upper left sleeve. *Stabsgefreiter* and *Oberstabsgefreiter* from July 1940 wore a four-pointed star above one or two inverted plaited braid chevrons on the upper left sleeve.
Leading seamen (*Maate*)	Foul anchor, or foul anchor above one inverted chevron on the upper left sleeve, and one or two silver (from 1.12.39 gold) lace stripes on the collar patches. Gold lace on the peacoat collar ends of working jackets.
Chief petty officers and petty officers	Pointed shoulder straps edged with lace and one to three four-pointed white metal stars. One narrow gold braid on the sun helmet.
Cadets (*Fähnriche*)	Flat aluminium braid shoulder cords with none or two four-pointed white metal stars. Two medium width gold braids on the sun helmet.
Lieutenants	One, two or two medium with one narrow lace ring between on the cuffs, and flat aluminium braid shoulder straps on dark blue ground with none to two four-pointed gilt metal stars. One row of gold zigzag embroidery on the cap peak. Two rows of gold braid on the sun helmet.
Captains	Three to four medium lace rings on the cuffs. From April 1944 *Fregattenkapitän* was to have worn three medium with one narrow underneath the uppermost ring, but this was seldom to be seen.

	Interwoven aluminium braid shoulder straps with none to two four-pointed gilt metal stars. One row of gold-embroidered oak leaves on the cap peak. Two rows of gold braid on sun helmet.
Commodores	One wide lace ring on the cuffs, and interwoven aluminium braid shoulder straps with two four-pointed gilt metal stars. Two rows of gold-embroidered oak leaves on the cap peak. Two rows of gold braid on the sun helmet.
Flag officers	One wide and one to three (*Generaladmiral* as C.-in-C. navy), four medium lace rings on the cuffs, and two gold and one silver interwoven braid shoulder straps on dark blue ground with none to three large four-pointed silver stars. *Grossadmiral* wore one wide and four medium lace rings, gold and silver braid shoulder straps with silver crossed batons. Two rows of gold-embroidered oak leaves on the cap peak.

All sea or executive officers (but not petty officers) and ratings were distinguished from personnel in other (*Laufbahn*) by the five-pointed star which was worn above the rank badges by all ranks. Petty officers wore their rating and branch badge combined on the upper left sleeve, while chief petty officers wore theirs on the shoulder straps.

Specialist training badges were embroidered in red on both white and blue uniforms, and were worn under the rating and branch badge on the left sleeve by seamen and petty officers.

Administrative officials wore silver badges, buttons, lace rings on the cuffs, with the branch badge above the rings, and on the shoulder straps. Officials with chief petty officer rank had silver lace on the shoulder straps, but later a new pattern with blue and silver interwoven braid was introduced.

From the middle of 1944 foreign personnel serving in the German navy began to receive a woven shield-shaped badge in their national colours for wear on the upper right sleeve.

Certain categories of naval personnel who served primarily on land such as coastal artillery were issued with field-grey service dress for wear on, and sometimes off, duty. Towards the end of the war there was a rapid build-up of naval personnel and civilians (*Frontwerftmänner*) into naval battalions, brigades and even divisions. Basic field-grey naval uniform is illustrated in 43–45.

On naval field-grey uniform rank was indicated in the army manner as follows:

Ratings	Yellow lace chevrons on dark green and later field-grey ground.
Petty officers	Pointed dark green and later field-grey cloth shoulder straps with gold lace and four-pointed white metal star. Gold lace on the tunic collar.
Officers	Army pattern matt aluminium braid shoulder straps on dark green underlay, and four-pointed gilt metal stars.
Flag officers	From 1944 army pattern gold and silver braid shoulder straps on dark or cornflower blue underlay, with large four-pointed silver stars. Army pattern collar patches with gold-embroidery on cornflower blue ground. It is not known for certain if flag officers had cornflower blue greatcoat lapels and *lampassen* on their grey breeches and trousers.

The branch of the wearer was indicated by the colour of the underlay on officer's shoulder straps, and by the badge worn on those shoulder straps as follows:

Branch	Colour	Badge
Generals	Cornflower blue	Branch badge.
Engineer officers	Dark green	Cogwheel
Doctors	Dark green	Aesculapius
Officials	—	As on blue uniform.
Personnel pool	Dark green	Crossed anchors and N (*Nordsee*) and O (*Ostsee*).
Air spotters	Dark green	Crossed lightning bolts and wings.
Naval artillery	Dark green	Anchor surmounted by flaming shell with numeral above.
Naval training battalion	Dark green	Crossed anchors.
Special naval battalion	Dark green	Crossed anchors for officers and crossed anchors and 's' for other ranks.
School for mates	Dark green	Crossed anchors then foul anchor.

German air force uniform was a development of that originally introduced in 1933 for members of the German Air Sport Association (*Deutscher-Luftsport-Verband*), which apart from its overt activities, was involved in the secret build-up of the new air force. Air force uniform was officially introduced in 1935, and remained virtually unchanged until the end of the war.

Officer's service dress is illustrated in 50 and 51, and other ranks in 72. With undress uniform (51) officers and senior n.c.o.s wore a dagger (239). It was worn on the left side suspended from two blue lace straps with aluminium wire edging, and white (generals gilt) metal fittings.

Generals and officials with general's rank had an undress double-breasted jacket with two rows of three gilt metal buttons, slanting side pockets with rounded flaps, and turn-back cuffs. The collar was edged in twisted gold cord, and the lapels and piping down the front and around the cuffs was in *Waffenfarbe*.

Between 1 April and 30 September officers and officials with officer's rank wore a peaked cap with white top, white tunic, which was identical in cut to the grey one, and either grey breeches and long trousers, or long white trousers and white canvas shoes. Other ranks could also wear the white cap cover, and long white trousers, but not the tunic.

The other ranks version of the service tunic was basically the same as the officers, but in November 1938 a new pattern, designed to be worn open or closed, began to replace it. The flying blouse for other ranks had at first no side pocket or national emblem, but in March 1940, blouses with these features began to be issued. Other ranks also wore a grey or white shirt, black tie, matching long trousers, and black leather footwear. The infantry pattern equipment, with rucksack instead of pack, was made of brown leather and grey canvas.

In addition to the uniforms illustrated in 64–66, paratroopers had an olive green duck training smock with no pockets, and smocks in basically the same cut but made in the following materials: plain olive, geometric army pattern camouflage, light (sand) khaki, and from 1943 onwards in the blurred predominantly brown army camouflage. Helmet covers were made usually of matching materials. Additional ammunition and flare cartridges were carried in canvas bandoliers made of grey, olive or camouflaged material.

The basic kinds of light khaki tropical clothing introduced in 1941 are illustrated in 58–60. Light khaki clothing was also worn in southern France, Italy, the Adriatic and southern Russia. The grey woollen greatcoat was also worn with tropical clothing (58).

Towards the end of 1942, surplus air force personnel were rapidly formed into ground combat formations, and thrown into action on the eastern front. They wore standard air force uniform, with the badges of their former unit, but because of the conspicuousness of the brightly coloured air force collar patches, these were often removed. All ranks began to wear their flying blouses and tunics closed at the neck. The only special items of clothing to be introduced were a three quarter-length single-breasted camouflage jacket (65) and in 1944 a field-grey field uniform, identical to the army pattern, but with the air force national emblem on the right breast.

Officers and n.c.o.s wore their rank badges on the collar patches and shoulder straps, and on the upper sleeves of their flying suits and jackets, and on the paratroop smock. Other ranks wore their rank badges on the upper left sleeve of their tunic, greatcoat, and overalls as follows:

Airmen	One to three aluminium lace inverted chevrons on the upper left sleeve, and one to four white metal wings on the collar patches. In May 1944 the rank of *Hauptgefreiter* (three chevrons and four wings) was changed to *Stabsgefreiter* with two chevrons and a four-pointed embroidered star, and four wings on the collar patches.
N.C.O.s	Aluminium lace on the shoulder straps, tunic and blouse collar, and greatcoat collar patches, and grey lace on the ends of the overall collar. One to four white metal wings on the collar patches and none to three white metal four-pointed stars on the shoulder straps. One to three, and three white lace stripes over a four-pointed star, on both sleeves of the overalls. *Hauptfeldwebel* or *Hauptwachtmeister* (or acting) two rows of aluminium or grey lace on both cuffs of all garments. One to four, and four white wings over a four-pointed star on both sleeves of flying suits and jackets, and paratroop smocks.
Junior officers	Collar patches edged in twisted aluminium cord and embroidered with oak leaves and one to three wings. Aluminium braid shoulder straps with none to two

gilt-metal four-pointed stars. One to three white wings over a white stripe on flying suits and jackets, and paratroop smocks.

Senior officers — Collar patches edged in twisted aluminium cord and embroidered with one to three wings within an open oak wreath. Interwoven aluminium braid shoulder straps with none to two gilt metal four-pointed stars. One to three white wings over two white stripes on flying suits, jackets and paratroop smocks.

General officers — Collar patches edged in twisted gold cord and embroidered with one to three gold wings within an open gold oak wreath. *Generaloberst* gold embroidered open oak wreath with superimposed gold air force national emblem. *Generalfeldmarschall* as for *Generaloberst* but with crossed silver batons at the base of the wreath. Two gold and one aluminium braid shoulder straps with none to three silver four-pointed stars. *Generalfeldmarschall* gold braid shoulder straps with crossed silver batons. One to three yellow wings above a yellow stripe for *Generalmajor*. *Generalleutnant* and *General*. *Generaloberst* yellow oak wreath with superimposed air force national emblem. *Generalfeldmarschall* as for *Generaloberst* but with white crossed batons at the base of the wreath, both on an oval ground.

Reich Marshal — From July 1940 Göring wore silver collar patches embroidered with gold laurel leaves around the edge, and with gold-embroidered national emblem in the centre of the right, and crossed batons in the centre of the left collar patch. From March 1941 crossed batons appeared on both collar patches. The shoulder straps were made of three gold braids with gilt metal crossed batons surmounted by the Reich eagle.

Officers in the administrative and engineering corps wore three-pointed stars on the shoulder straps and two to four-bladed propellers instead of wings on their collar patches. In November 1940 engineer officers were also entitled to wear wings, and although the collar patches with propellers were abolished they continued to be worn.

Waffenfarben appeared on other ranks peaked caps, on collar patches, and shoulder straps of all ranks, on the collar cord of other ranks, on the greatcoat and undress jacket lapels and piping, and as *lampassen* on the breeches and trousers of general officers as follows:

Branch	Colour
Generals and Regiment General Göring and brigade and divisional H.Q.s	White
General staff	Crimson
Flying personnel, parachute troops and units and schools without own colour	Golden yellow
Signals	Golden brown
Anti-aircraft artillery and ordnance	Scarlet
Engineer corps and engineer officers*	Pink
Medical	Cornflower blue
Air traffic control	Bright green
Administrative officials and navigation experts	Dark green
Construction troops	Black

*from 1940

A new system was introduced in January 1943 for members of the air force field formations. The collar patches were rifle green with twisted aluminium cord for officers and piping in *Waffenfarbe* for other ranks. Shoulder straps for officers had a *Waffenfarbe* underlay, and those for other ranks *Waffenfarbe* piping.

Branch	Colour
Rifle regiments and guard companies	Rifle green
Bicycle companies	Golden yellow
Recce. companies	Golden yellow
Artillery regiments	Scarlet
Anti-aircraft battalions	Scarlet
Anti-tank gun units	Pink
Signals battalions	Golden brown
Engineer battalions	Black

Members of Göring's personal regiment, which by the end of the war had been expanded into a Parachute Tank Corps, wore air force uniform with white *Waffenfarbe*, and originally green piping around the white collar patches for members of the rifle, and scarlet piping for members of the anti-aircraft battalions. At the beginning of 1943 the system was changed and all ranks in all units wore white collar patches without coloured piping (officers retained the aluminium cord) and coloured piping appeared thereafter on the shoulder straps.

Arm	*Colour*
Divisional staff, tank regiment and assault gun battalion	Pink
Grenadier regiments and guard regiment	White
Rifle regiment	Rifle green
Armoured Recce. batt. and *Flugbereitschaft*	Golden yellow
Artillery regiments and anti-aircraft battalions	Scarlet
Signals battalions	Golden brown
Engineer battalions	Black
Supply, administration and field gendarmerie	Light blue
Field gendarmerie from June 1943	Orange

Members of the tank regiment and assault gun battalion at first wore black army pattern *Panzer* collar patches piped in white and also possibly pink, with the white metal death's head, but later this pattern was replaced by white air force collar patches with the same death's head.

In addition to the *Waffenfarbe* the corps or branch was also indicated by a badge on the shoulder straps. These badges were in gilt metal for officers, white metal for generals and senior n.c.o.s and in *Waffenfarbe* embroidery for other ranks. Specialists and tradesmen with non-commissioned rank wore a silver-grey machine-embroidered badge on the lower left sleeve.

Foreign personnel serving in the air force formations such as the Croatian Air Force Legion, and the air contingent of the Spanish 'Blue Division' (62) wore German uniform with a woven shield-shaped badge in their national colours on the upper right sleeve, and pilots and observers continued to wear their flying badges on German uniform, usually in the same position as it was worn on their national uniform.

Auxiliary organisations which served alongside the air force, were the Air Force Fire Service, whose personnel wore German fire service blue uniform with air force cap badges and national emblem on the right breast, and administrative officials rank badges for officers, and a special system for firemen who were technically civilian employees.

Members of the National Socialist Motor Transport Corps (*N.S.K.K.*) and Technical Emergency Service (*Technische Nothilfe*) serving with the air force in occupied territories wore air force uniform with the insignia and rank badges of their respective organisations. As the air war on Germany increased, German and foreign youths were recruited as Anti-Aircraft Helpers (*Flakhelfer*), and Air Force Helpers (*Luftwaffenhelfer*), and elderly men joined the Homeland Anti-Aircraft Corps (*Heimatflak*). Youths were issued with grey versions of the Hitler Youth uniform with a light blue air force national emblem ensigned by the letters LH on a triangular black ground, on the right breast, and Hitler Youth rank badges on the shoulder straps, which were piped in light blue. Foreign youths wore a cap badge in the shape of a rhomboid, and armlet in their national colours. Members of the *Heimatflak* wore air force uniform without rank badges or national emblem.

GREAT BRITAIN   Royal Navy

British naval uniform as worn during World War 2 dates from the middle of the last century, while the wartime rating's uniform was a development of that originally introduced in 1857.

The basic service dress for officers is illustrated in 74. The greatcoat was double-breasted with stand-and-fall collar which could be worn open or closed, two rows of six gilt metal buttons, slash side pockets with straight flaps, and sword slit above the left pocket. The back had two vertical flaps and a half-belt with a button at each end. There was also a blue version of the double-breasted 'British warm'.

Officer's 'whites' are illustrated in 77, but not shown is the white sun helmet with white puggree which had a $\frac{1}{4}$ in. blue flash showing at the top. In February 1938 a new tropical dress consisting of white shirt, white shorts, white stockings and canvas shoes, or black stockings and black leather shoes was introduced. There was also a khaki service dress with peaked cap cover, single-breasted tunic with four buttons, and patch pockets, and matching long trousers. It was worn with khaki shirt and tie, and either blue shoulder straps with gold lace rank distinctions, or khaki lace cuff rings.

During the war officers increasingly wore khaki drill clothing in the tropics (76), and towards the end of the war in the Far East they also adopted jungle green clothing.

Chief petty officers uniforms were basically the same as officers except that they had a special cap badge, and they wore their rating badge on the sleeve. For everyday wear chief petty officers wore the uniform illustrated in 75, but with three buttons on the cuffs. This same basic uniform was also worn by petty officers, and miscellaneous junior ratings who were not members of the seamen branch. Chief petty officers, petty officers, and miscellaneous junior ratings also wore in the summer months or in the tropics, a white cap cover, single-breasted white tunic with stand-collar, open patch breast pockets and four brass (junior ratings black plastic) buttons, long white trousers and white canvas shoes. Junior ratings wore black leather shoes.

Ratings in the seamen branch wore a white shirt with mid blue dungarees binding round the neck opening, white jumper with blue binding around the cuffs and skirt, and the same mid-blue collar, black scarf or 'silk', and white knife (Pusser's dirk) lanyard as with the blue jumper. Hat with white cover and black leather shoes completed the uniform.

The Class II uniform for ratings and unconfirmed petty officers with less than one year's service is illustrated in 73. The greatcoat (84) for all ratings was single-breasted with fall collar, which could be worn open or closed, five black plastic buttons in front, and adjustable belt at the back. There was also a double-breasted blue gabardine raincoat in civilian cut.

In February 1938 a new tropical dress (78) was introduced which included a white sun helmet, on the front of which chief petty officers and petty officers wore a yellow metal cap badge, short-sleeved shirt open at the neck, white shorts, white woollen stockings and white canvas shoes. Miscellaneous junior ratings wore black stockings and black leather shoes. Seamen ratings wore the same basic uniform but with the same shirt with blue binding at the neck, as was worn under the white jumper.

During the war the most common form of tropical dress was the white-topped hat, or khaki drill sun helmet, khaki drill shirt, or Royal Marine pattern tunic, and khaki drill long or short trousers. Wartime additions to naval uniform were the khaki battle-dress (86–87) which was first introduced in 1941 for officers, and later for all ratings serving in certain shore installations and on combined operations. In October

1943 a battle-dress type blue uniform was approved as a working dress (83).

Some examples of the many different kinds of working dress are illustrated in 79–81.

Rank was indicated by the number and width of gold lace rings, which from August 1941, began to be worn only half-way round the cuff. Gold lace (later woven yellow) stripes on the blue shoulder straps, and on blue or khaki slides on khaki battle-dress and khaki drill clothing, and sometimes painted or transferred on the front and back of the steel helmet. Ratings wore their badges on the upper left sleeve. Members of Naval Beach Parties painted their rating badge in yellow on the front of the steel helmet, and also wore them in blue on white armlets on the left arm.

Leading seamen	Foul anchor on the upper left sleeve, and sometimes on the front of the helmet. Peaked cap badge embroidered in blue worsted.
Petty officers	Crossed foul anchors ensigned by a crown on the upper left sleeve and sometimes on the steel helmet. Peaked cap badge embroidered in gold.
Chief petty officers	Three buttons on the outside of the cuffs, and special cap badge embroidered in gold with open laurel wreath.
Cadets	Braid loop in white for regular navy, blue for R.N.R., and maroon for R.N.V.R., with a small brass button on the ends of the jacket collar on both sides. Sometimes cadets wore three small buttons on blue shoulder straps on the working tunic.
Midshipmen	Gorget patches in white for regular navy, blue for R.N.R., and maroon for R.N.V.R. with a small brass button on the jacket collar on both sides.
Warrant officers	One $\frac{1}{4}$ in. or one $\frac{1}{2}$ in. gold lace ring with curl on the cuffs and shoulder straps.
Lieutenants and Lieut. Commanders	One or two medium with one narrow 'half stripe' between, with a curl on the only or uppermost, on the cuffs and shoulder straps.
Captains and Commanders	Three or four medium gold lace rings with a curl on the uppermost on the cuffs and shoulder

	straps. One row of gold oak leaves on the cap peak.
Commodore 2nd class	One wide gold lace ring with a medium gold lace circle above, on the cuffs and shoulder straps, and one row of gold oakleaves on the cap peak.
Commodores 1st class	One wide with one medium gold lace ring above with a curl on the cuffs. Gold lace shoulder straps with silver-embroidered crown, two silver-embroidered eight-pointed stars (side by side) and foul anchor. Peak embroidered all round with gold oak leaves.
Rear admirals	One wide with one medium gold lace ring above with a curl on the cuffs. Gold lace shoulder straps with silver-embroidered crown, one large eight-pointed star ensigned by crossed baton and sword. Peak embroidered all round with oak leaves.
Vice admirals	One wide with two medium gold lace rings above with a curl on the uppermost, on the cuffs. Gold lace shoulder straps with silver-embroidered crown, two small eight-pointed stars ensigned by crossed baton and sword. Peak embroidered all round with oak leaves.
Admirals	One wide and three medium gold lace rings above, with a curl on the uppermost, on the cuffs. Gold lace shoulder straps with silver embroidered crown, three eight-pointed stars, ensigned by crossed baton and sword. Peak embroidered all round with oak leaves.
Admiral of the Fleet	One wide with four medium gold lace rings above, with a curl on the uppermost, on the cuffs. Gold lace shoulder straps with silver-embroidered crown above an open laurel wreath with crossed batons in the centre. Peak embroidered all round with gold oak leaves.

Members of the civil branches (non-executive officers) were identified by coloured backing or 'lights' to the lace rank distinctions as follows:

Branch	Colour
Engineers	Purple
Surgeons	Scarlet
Dentists	Orange
Accountants	White
Instructors	Light blue
Shipwright and constructors	Silver grey
Ordnance officers	Royal blue
Electrical officers	Light green

Cadets and midshipmen wore a strip of cloth in the above colours on their shoulder straps.

Specialist badges were as follows:

Rate	Badge	Uniform	Position
C.P.O.	Gold	Blue dress	Collar
	Red	Blue working	Collar
	Gold	White	Right cuff
P.O.s & seamen	Gold	Blue dress	Right sleeve
	Red	Blue working	Right sleeve
	Light blue	White	Right sleeve

The following branches and specialist roles were distinguished by the following badges:

Fleet Air Arm	Gold embroidered 'A' inside the curl of the rank distinction lace. Gold-embroidered pilot and observer wings worn on the left cuff above the curl on the blue uniform jacket, and on the left breast on all other tunics.
Royal Naval Reserve	Each ring made of plaited lace ($\frac{3}{4}$ in. wide) with blue showing between. The narrow or 'half stripe' was straight. Cadets and midshipmen wore blue loops and collar patches respectively.
Royal Naval Volunteer Reserve	Each ring made of waved lace. From 1941 the half stripe was also to be waved and not straight. Cadets and midshipmen wore maroon loops or collar patches. Letters R.N.V.R. some-

	times worn on cuff above buttons by chief petty officers.
Combined Operations	Red anchor ensigned by a winged bird and crossed with a Thompson gun on a blue ground worn on both sleeves at shoulder height.
Naval Beach Parties	Blue shoulder flashes with either 'Royal Navy' or 'Beach Signals' in white on both sleeves at shoulder height. Armlet, worn on upper left arm or sometimes on the left cuff, with the letters N.B.P.
Guard duty	White armlet edged in blue with blue crown.
Naval police	White armlet edged in blue with blue crown and letters N and P.

GREAT BRITAIN   Royal Marines

The Royal Marines were permanently established in April 1755, and by the outbreak of World War 2 had a strength of some 12,000 men. In February 1942, the first of nine Royal Marine commandos was formed. Officers wore an open single-breasted blue tunic or frock, with four gilt metal buttons, matching shoulder straps with gilt metal rank badges above the letters RM, pleated patch breast pockets with three-pointed flap and button, and pointed cuffs with two small buttons at the back. The corps 'globe and laurel' badge in gilt and silvered metal was worn on the ends of the collar on both sides. The tunic was worn with blue whistle lanyard looped over the left shoulder, white shirt, black tie, matching long trousers with scarlet piping, black leather shoes, brown leather gloves, brown leather 'Sam Browne' belt, and army officers pattern khaki greatcoat.

The peaked cap was blue with scarlet band and piping around the crown, black leather chin strap, and peak, which was embroidered with gold oak leaves for field officers. During the war the white piqué cover was only worn in the tropics. The side cap was blue with scarlet piping and two small gilt buttons in front and collar badge on left side. The cap badge was in gilt and silvered metal for officers; colonel and above wore corresponding gold-embroidered army pattern cap badges. The white universal pattern Wolseley helmet (91) was still worn with certain orders of dress during the war. On all occasions when the helmet's ball top was not in use, a white cloth covered zinc button was worn instead.

Officers also wore army pattern khaki service dress with bronzed buttons and badges. Tropical clothing included a khaki drill tunic and trousers in the same cut as the blue, which was worn with gilt metal buttons and badges, as well as a light khaki tennis pattern shirt with collar attached and patch breast pockets, matching shorts, khaki stockings or puttees, and brown leather shoes or black leather ankle boots.

The basic other ranks uniform with Wolseley helmet is illustrated in 91. During the war a utility tunic with plain patch breast pockets, and no side pockets was introduced. Marines received two pair of scarlet-piped trousers, and one pair of plain blue serge working trousers. The greatcoat was either the special khaki marine or standard army pattern. Other ranks head-dress included a blue peaked cap with scarlet band, and scarlet piping around the crown for quartermaster sergeants, black peak and chin strap, and brass badge. In summer in home waters until April 1940, and throughout the war in the tropics, marines wore the white duck cap, with white top, scarlet band, and black peak and chin strap, and brass badge.

Tropical dress consisted of khaki drill tunic and trousers in similar cut to the blue uniform, but during the war shirt-sleeve order as illustrated in 93 was most common. Other items were the universal pattern helmet in light khaki with flash in Royal Marine colours on the left side, or the army pattern khaki helmet with puggree for wear in the East Indies or Singapore, khaki side cap, khaki drill shorts, khaki woollen stockings or drab hose tops.

Army pattern khaki service dress was replaced at the beginning of the war by standard army khaki battle-dress, which was worn with khaki 'field-service' side cap. Badges and buttons for other ranks were in brass on khaki service dress, but on battle-dress the straight red and blue 'Royal Marine' shoulder flash was the only distinctive insignia. During the war a number of formation flashes were introduced for wear on battle-dress. In February 1942 long puttees were replaced by short ones, and beginning in 1943 crews of landing craft were issued with blue battle-dress (92). Blue battle-dress was later issued to Royal Marines Ships detachments, and the blue beret gradually replaced all other types of head-dress, until it became standard issue at the end of 1943.

Royal Marine commandos wore battle-dress with straight woven blue shoulder flashes with 'Royal Marines', the number of the Commando (40–48) above, and 'Commando' below, all in red. From 1943 commandos wore the green beret and in action the camouflaged 'Denison' smock.

Rank was indicated as in the army, except that on the greatcoat the chevrons were worn on the cuffs. Other ranks wore the following rank badges:

Lance corporal	One chevron.
Corporal	Two chevrons.
Sergeant	Three chevrons.
Colour sergeant	Three chevrons surmounted by a crown.
Quartermaster sergeant	Crown in laurel wreath.
Regimental Sergeant Major	Royal arms.
Warrant officer	Letters wo within open laurel wreath on the shoulder straps.

Chevrons were worn on the right sleeve of the blue, and on both sleeves of khaki uniforms. On blue uniform the chevrons were red, and white on khaki ground (including officer's stars and crowns) on khaki uniforms.

GREAT BRITAIN   Royal Air Force

The grey or 'French blue' (as it was originally called) uniform was introduced in 1919, and was to form the model for air force uniforms throughout the world.

Service dress for officers and other ranks is illustrated in 98 and the greatcoat for officers in 122. There was also a grey raincoat with fly-front, matching belt, cuff tabs, and no insignia. Other ranks also had a double-breasted greatcoat with two rows of four brass, and slanting side pockets with flap. The peaked cap was grey with black mohair band, black leather peak and chin strap, and gold-embroidered cap badge for officers, and brass for other ranks. Air or general officers had the peak embroidered all round with gold oak leaves, while senior officers had one row only. In 1940 the air force tried the battle-dress, and in 1943 a grey version was generally introduced as a working dress. It differed from the army pattern only in that the flaps of the breast pockets were three-pointed and not just pointed.

Before the war in the tropics personnel wore the Wolseley helmet with puggree and flash in the R.A.F. colours on the left side, or the pith hat in India, khaki drill tunic, shirt, tie, short or long trousers, khaki woollen stockings and black shoes or boots. During the war in the Middle East officers wore the bushjacket (101), and in the Far East towards the end of the war they also adopted jungle green clothing (100) and the 'wide awake' or slouch hat.

Rank was indicated on the cuffs of the grey tunic for officers, and on grey shoulder straps on the grey greatcoat, battle-dress blouse, and on tropical tunics and shirts. Other ranks wore their rank badges on the upper left sleeve. With grey uniform rank badges were embroidered or woven in light blue on black ground, and chevrons were embroidered in blue worsted on black ground. On tropical uniforms rank badges were embroidered or woven in red on light khaki ground, and chevrons were either the army pattern embroidered in white worsted on khaki ground, or made of white tape for wear on shirts. Both officers and other ranks wore their rank badges on dark blue armlets when wearing working overalls, and n.c.o.s also wore their rank badges in this manner with shirt-sleeve order.

Rank was indicated as follows:

Leading Aircraftsmen	Twin-bladed propeller on upper left sleeve.
N.C.O.s	Two or three inverted chevrons. Flight sergeant three inverted chevrons surmounted by brass crown on upper left sleeve.
Warrant Officers	Royal arms on lower right sleeve.
Junior officers	One narrow, or one or two medium rings of black and light blue lace on the cuffs and shoulder straps.
Senior officers	Two medium with one narrow between, or three or four medium rings of black and light blue lace on the cuffs, and shoulder straps. One row of gold-embroidered oak leaves on the cap peak.
General (air) officers	One row of wide black and light blue lace, with none to four medium rings above on the cuffs and shoulder straps. Peak embroidered all round with gold oak leaves.

A number of branches and specialist roles in the R.A.F. were distinguished by special collar badges and armlets, some of which appear in the illustrations.

Personnel of many nationalities served with the R.A.F. either in national formations, or in those of the R.A.F., and their nationality was identifiable by the shoulder flash which bore the name of their country, or initials if it happened to be a long one, e.g. 's.l.b.w.a.' for Sierra Leone British West Africa. The American Eagle Squadron had the American eagle surmounted by the letters 'e' and 's' in light blue on a grey ground. Members of the Polish and Norwegian air forces wore a number of national features on their R.A.F. uniform, but these will be dealt with in the sections dealing with the respective country.

In 1944 R.A.F. Servicing Commandos were formed for the invasion of Normandy. Their task was to put captured airfields into use without delay, and to service and refuel aircraft which had to land at forward airstrips. They wore R.A.F. battle-dress and rank badges, and the combined operations flash on the upper left sleeve.

Royal Air Force Regiment

The Royal Air Force Regiment was formed in February 1942 from various armoured car and other land-based units of the R.A.F. Its primary role was the defence and security of forward airfields, but towards the end of the war in Europe took on more aggressive roles. Its personnel wore R.A.F. service dress for ceremonial occasions, and army uniform in action, with dark blue shoulder flashes edged in light blue with 'R.A.F. Regiment' in light blue as illustrated in 111.

Royal Observer Corps

The Observer Corps was formed in 1918, and in 1929 became part of the Royal Air Force under the Air Ministry. In April 1941 the 30,000 strong corps was granted the royal warrant, and became the Royal Observer Corps.

In June 1941, the blue and white vertically striped armlet with 'Observer Corps' in red letters, was changed for a grey serge battle-dress uniform (112). In addition to the black beret, a black steel helmet, on the front of which was sometimes painted 'Observer Corps' in white, was worn when on duty.

Officers wore R.A.F. uniform with special metal cap badge, and the letters ROC in gilt metal on the ends of the collar on both sides. In March 1943, the rectangular woven badges bearing the words 'Head Observer' and 'Duty Controller' which were worn on the left breast pocket flap, and the black lace ring which denoted officer status were replaced by a new system of rank badges as follows:

Leading observers	Two horizontal light blue embroidered bars within a light blue open laurel wreath on dark blue ground, on both upper sleeves.
Chief observers	As above but with three bars.
Observer lieutenants	One or two medium, or two medium blue lace rings with one narrow between, on the cuffs and shoulder straps.
Observer captains and commanders	Three or four medium blue lace rings on the cuffs and shoulder straps.
Observer commodore	One wide blue lace ring on the cuffs and shoulder straps.

In January 1944 master spotters were distinguished by a light blue Spitfire on a blue circular ground, which was worn on the left sleeve. In May 1944 members of the R.O.C. were attached to ships of the invasion fleet, and were known as 'aircraft identifiers', and were rated as petty officers. They wore R.O.C. uniform with a dark blue shoulder flash with 'Seaborne' in light blue letters, on both sleeves at shoulder height, and a rectangular dark blue cloth badge with the letters 'R.N.' in light blue on the upper left sleeve at elbow height.

Between the wars a number of organisations were formed to train young boys for service in the R.A.F. The Air Defence Corps was started in 1938, and cadets wore standard R.A.F. uniform with special chrome cap badge, and cloth Royal Ensign on the upper left sleeve. Officers sometimes wore a chrome 'C' on the ends of the collar on both sides, and above the rank distinction lace on the shoulder straps. Officers wore silver rank distinction lace.

The Civil Air Guard was established between the wars to encourage pilot training. Its personnel wore a blue boiler suit, dark blue side cap with chrome badge, and the ensign arm badge of the Air Defence Corps. In February 1941 the Air Defence Cadet Corps was absorbed by the newly formed Air Training Corps or A.T.C. Cadets wore R.A.F. uniform with special cap badge (114). Officers wore R.A.F. uniform with 'V.R.'

(Volunteer Reserve) on the ends of the collar on both sides and on the shoulder straps. In 1944 the 'v.r.' was changed to a crown-less version of the cap badge in gilt metal. Officers wore R.A.F. rank badges, with above the letters 'ATC' within a ring in light blue on a dark blue ground. Cadets had their own system of rank stars, propellers and inverted chevrons.

AUSTRALIA   Royal Australian Navy

R.A.N. came into existence as a fleet in 1913. Uniform was as for Royal Navy (74) but with Australian buttons; hat ribbon with 'H.M.A.S.' etc. Australians serving with Royal Navy wore 'Australia' shoulder flashes.

Royal Australian Air Force

The A.A.F. was formed on 31 March 1931, and granted the Royal Warrant in August 1941. Its personnel wore dark blue uniforms (115) with gold rank distinction lace ensigned by a gilt metal eagle. The blue uniform as well as blue battle-dress continued to be worn during the war, but the gold lace was often replaced by the R.A.F. pattern. Australians serving with the R.A.F. wore the 'Australia' flash.

CANADA   Royal Canadian Navy

Formed in 1910 with Royal Navy uniform, but with Canadian buttons, and hat ribbon 'H.M.C.S.' etc. Canadians serving with Royal Navy wore 'Canada' shoulder flashes.

Royal Canadian Air Force

The Canadian Air Force was granted the Royal Warrant in 1924. With the exception of special winter and flying clothing (118), uniform was that of the R.A.F. Canadians serving in the R.A.F. wore the 'Canada' shoulder flash. Americans serving in the R.C.A.F. wore 'u.s.a.' under the 'Canada' flash.

INDIA   Royal Indian Navy

The Royal Indian Marine Service became the R.I.N. in October 1934, and by 1943 had some twenty thousand men. Uniform was as for the Royal Navy but with Indian cap badge and buttons, and 'H.M.I.S.' hat tally. On racial or religious grounds a puggree could be worn with prescribed cap badge or hat tally (96).

Indian Air Force

The I.A.F. was formed in 1933, and served throughout the war in India. Only selected personnel sent to Europe for training received the grey uniform of the R.A.F. on which they wore 'India' shoulder flashes, and the 'v.r.' of the volunteer reserve. The basic dress worn in India was the khaki drill tropical dress of the R.A.F. The strength of the I.A.F. in 1943 was 30,000 men.

NEW ZEALAND   Royal New Zealand Navy

The R.N.Z.N. was formed in 1920. Its personnel wore the uniform of the Royal Navy with New Zealand buttons, and hat ribbon 'H.M.N.Z.S.' etc. New Zealanders serving with the Royal Navy wore the 'New Zealand' flash.

Royal New Zealand Air Force

Originally formed in June 1923, the New Zealand Permanent Air Force received its Royal Warrant in February 1934. R.A.F. rank titles were introduced in 1929, and the grey uniform, for special occasions, in 1931. In 1937 the R.N.Z.A.F. became a separate service. New Zealanders serving with the R.A.F. wore the 'New Zealand' flash (106).

SOUTH AFRICA   South African Naval Service

Uniform was as for the Royal Navy but with South African buttons, and standard hat ribbon with foul anchor between letters 's' and 'A'. Reserve and Volunteer Reserve officers wore the same straight rank distinction lace as regular officers. South Africans serving with the Royal Navy wore the 'South Africa' flash.

Royal South African Air Force

Formed in February 1920 as part of the army. Its personnel wore army uniforms with bronzed badges. South Africans serving with the R.A.F. wore grey uniform with 'South Africa' flash (117).

GREECE   Royal Hellenic Navy

Since the uniform of the Greek navy was almost identical to that of the Royal Navy, it will only be described here in so far as it differed from the British pattern.

For officers and petty officers service dress see 124–25.

In addition to the blue, white and light khaki uniforms, there was also a khaki winter uniform with khaki coloured lace rings to indicate rank.

Rank was indicated as follows:

Seamen 2nd and 1st Class	One or two red tape chevrons on the upper sleeves.
Petty officers	One narrow, one wide, one narrow and one wide, and two wide gold lace chevrons on the upper sleeves.
Warrant officers	A gold lace chevron above one medium, one medium and one narrow gold lace rings on the cuffs, and shoulder straps.
Lieutenants	One or two medium, or two medium with one narrow between, gold lace rings with a curl on the only or uppermost on the cuffs and shoulder straps.
Captains and Commanders	Three medium, three medium with one narrow, or four medium gold lace rings with a curl on the

	uppermost on the cuffs and shoulder straps. One row of gold-embroidered oak leaves on the cap peak.
Flag officers	One wide with one to three medium gold lace rings above with a curl on the uppermost, on the cuffs. Gold lace shoulder straps with silver-embroidered crown above crossed sword and baton and one to three silver stars beneath. Two rows of gold embroidered oak leaves on the cap peak.
Admiral of the Fleet	This rank was held by the reigning monarch who wore one wide with four medium gold lace rings above, with a curl on the uppermost, on the cuffs. Gold lace shoulder straps with silver crowned royal cypher with crossed batons within a laurel wreath beneath.

As in the Royal Navy officers served either in the line, reserve or volunteer reserve and wore the same distinctive pattern of lace rings and curls as their British counterparts.

The various branches or corps wore different colours between the lace on the cuff and shoulder strap (which do not have the curl) as follows:

Branch	Colour
Engineers	Dark violet velvet
Naval construction/Dockyard	Black velvet
Electrical engineers	Light violet velvet
Doctors	Crimson
Harbour masters	Anchor instead of curl above the rank distinction lace.
Legal officers	Violet
Supply officers	White
Pharmacists	Green velvet
Paymasters	Scarlet velvet
Research chemists	Light green velvet

Trade and specialist badges were worn as follows:

Rating/rank	Badge colour	Position
Commissioned warrant officers	Gold	Above curls.
Warrant officers	Gold	Above angle of chevrons.

Petty officers	Gold	Inside angle of chevrons.
Seamen	Red	Inside angle of chevrons or in corresponding position.

Members of the submarine service wore a gilt metal submarine above the left breast pocket.

GREECE   Royal War Aviation

The air force was formed in 1923, and by the outbreak of World War 2, its personnel were wearing a grey service dress which resembled that of Great Britain.

Officers wore an open single-breasted grey tunic with four gilt metal buttons in front, pleated patch breast and patch side pockets with three-pointed flap and button. It was worn with white or grey shirt and black tie, matching long trousers, and black leather shoes. The greatcoat was double-breasted.

The peaked cap was grey with black mohair band, black leather peak and chin strap, and embroidered badge.

In hot weather officers wore khaki drill.

Other ranks uniform is illustrated in 126.

Rank was indicated as follows:

Corporals	One inverted yellow lace chevron. Corporal A one inverted yellow lace chevron with the letter 'A' in the vertex, on the upper sleeves.
Sergeants	Two or three inverted yellow lace chevrons on the upper sleeves.
Warrant Officers	One narrow blue lace ring with a chevron above and joined to it, on the cuffs.
Junior officers	One, two, or two medium with one narrow blue lace ring between, with a rhomboid on the only or uppermost ring, on the cuffs.
Senior officers	Three, three medium and one narrow, or four blue lace rings with a rhomboid on the uppermost, on the cuffs. One row of gold-embroidered oak leaves on the cap peak.
General officers	One wide and one to four medium blue lace rings

with a rhomboid on the uppermost on the cuffs, and
gold-embroidered oak leaves all round the cap
peak.

HUNGARY   Royal Hungarian River Forces

The original river guard was formed in 1922 by the Ministry of the
Interior to police the Danube river, but later it was transferred to the
Ministry of War.

Officers wore blue full dress, and khaki service dress as illustrated in
128. The khaki greatcoat was double-breasted with two rows of six gilt
metal buttons, and side pockets with straight flaps, and turn-back cuffs
with three small buttons on the outside seam at the back. Officers also
wore a long khaki cape with brown velvet collar. The peaked cap was
khaki with lighter khaki fabric band, and gold-embroidered cap badge –
open oak wreath with foul anchor in the centre ensigned by the crown of
St Stephen. The peak was brown lacquered leather and the chin strap was
made of gold cords. Other ranks wore a single-breasted open khaki tunic
with four bronzed (n.c.o.s silver) buttons, pleated patch breast, and
patch side pockets with straight flap and button, three small buttons at
the back of the cuff, and matching shoulder straps with roll or parolli.
Under the tunic ratings wore a khaki vest, and large rectangular white
collar, while senior n.c.o.s wore a khaki shirt and tie.

The hat was khaki with black silk ribbon and *M. Kir. Honvèd Folyam-
ierök* in silver wire letters. The ribbon was worn long and the ends hung
down at the back of the neck. Above the ribbon on the front of the hat
was worn a bronzed metal version of the officers cap badge. Senior n.c.o.s
wore a khaki peaked cap with lighter fabric band, silver embroidered cap
badge, silver chin cords and brown peak.

Ratings wore a brown leather waist belt with plain steel buckle and
bayonet with brown wooden grip and khaki sheath. All other equipment
was the standard infantry pattern.

Officers wore their rank distinction lace on the tunic cuffs, and in a
shortened form on the outside of the greatcoat cuffs. Ratings wore their
rank badges on the cuffs. The first pattern, which consisted of a pointed
rectangular blue cloth patch edged with brown or silver cord, with a
loop at the top three corners, was replaced by June 1942 by a simpler
system of lace bars.

Rank was indicated as follows:

Other ranks — Vertical pointed blue cloth patch edged with narrow brown cord with loops at the top three corners. On the patch were none to three six-pointed white bone or plastic stars. Then none to three blue tape bars on the cuffs.

N.C.O.s — Vertical pointed blue cloth patch edged with narrow silver cord with loops at the top three corners. On the patch were one to three six-pointed white metal stars under a silver lace chevron. Then one to three narrow silver lace bars.

Warrant officers — As for n.c.o.s but with gold lace bar with one six-pointed gilt metal star on it. Then one silver with one narrow gold lace bar above on the cuffs.

Ensign — One very narrow gold lace stripe with curl on the outside of the cuffs only.

Junior officers — One to three narrow gold lace rings (bars on the greatcoat) with a small curl on the only or uppermost ring, on the cuffs.

Senior officers — One medium zigzag-pattern gold lace ring with one to three narrow gold lace rings above with a curl on the uppermost, on the cuffs. One row of gold braid on the front edge of the cap peak.

Generals — Gold-embroidered open oak wreath with the Holy Crown of St Stephen in the centre, above one or two narrow gold lace rings with a curl on the uppermost, and one wide zigzag-pattern gold lace ring, on the cuffs. One row of gold-embroidered oak leaves on the cap peak.

The various branches were distinguished by the following colours between the rank distinction lace. Only line officers had the curl.

Branch	Colour
Engineers	Cherry cloth
Constructors	Cherry cloth
Surgeons	Black velvet
Paymasters	Green cloth
Directors of Music	Violet cloth

The air force was originally formed in 1919, in contradiction to the Versailles Treaty, so its first personnel were employed by the Ministry of Communications, and did not wear uniform. By the outbreak of the war the air force had been considerably expanded, and its personnel dressed in a khaki service dress.

The basic uniform for officers is illustrated in 127. The greatcoat was double-breasted with large fall-collar and two rows of six buttons. The peaked cap was khaki with brown leather peak, gold piping around the bottom of the band for officers, and twisted gold chin cord. The winged crown cap badge was embroidered in gold for officers and silver for senior n.c.o.s on a black cloth ground. In hot weather officers and senior n.c.o.s wore a light khaki service dress, and on active duty shirt-sleeve order was permitted.

Other ranks uniform is illustrated in 129.

Winter flying suits were made of black or brown leather with zip-fasteners, pack-type parachute, and goggles, while in summer pilots wore shirt-sleeve order and canvas flying helmet, or one-piece beige canvas flying suit.

Rank was indicated on the shoulder straps for all ranks on the tunic, and on the shoulder straps for officers, and on the cuffs for other ranks on the greatcoat. In addition flying officers and n.c.o.s wore rectangular patches in the same colours, and bearing the same rank distinctions as on the shoulder straps, on both cuffs of the flying suit and jacket. All officers had gold, n.c.o.s silver, and other ranks bronzed buttons and badges.

Rank was indicated as follows:

Airmen	One inverted narrow white tape chevron, or same chevron above on white tape stripe across the black cloth shoulder straps, and one black lace bar on the greatcoat cuffs.
Junior n.c.o.s	One inverted narrow silver lace chevron above two or three narrow silver lace stripes across the black cloth shoulder straps. Two or three black lace bars on the greatcoat cuffs.
Senior n.c.o.s	One inverted medium silver lace chevron above one to three medium silver lace stripes across the black cloth shoulder straps piped in silver.

Warrant officers	Staff sergeant: One inverted medium gold lace chevron above one medium gold lace stripe on black cloth shoulder straps piped in silver.
Ensigns	One inverted medium gold lace chevron above one medium gold lace stripe on black cloth shoulder straps piped in gold.
Junior officers	One inverted medium gold lace chevron above one to three medium gold lace stripes on the shoulder straps and cuff patch, which were piped in gold.
Senior officers	One inverted medium gold lace chevron above one to three medium and one wide gold zigzag-pattern lace stripes on the shoulder straps and cuff patches, which were piped in gold.
Generals	One or two medium, above one very wide gold zigzag-pattern lace stripes on scarlet shoulder straps or cuff patches, which were piped in gold. Open gold-embroidered oak wreath around the shoulder strap button. Scarlet *lampassen* on breeches and trousers.

The following branches of the air force were distinguished by the following colours which appeared on the shoulder straps:

Corps	Shoulder straps	Distinction
Generals	Scarlet	Oak wreath.
General staff	Gold rank distinction lace mounted on black cloth on scarlet shoulder strap	Inverted chevron.
Technical General Staff	Cherry velvet	Inverted chevron.
Engineering	Green cloth	No chevron.
Band	Mauve cloth	No chevron.

ITALY   Royal and Republican Navies

The Italian navy came into existence in 1860 with the unification of the Sardinian and Neopolitan fleets together with other elements. Uniforms worn during World War 2 were the result of regulations issued on 1 February 1936.

Officer's service dress is illustrated in 131 and petty officers (*Capo*) wore basically the same. In addition to the peaked cap there was a blue field cap with matching cloth peak, and reduced version of the cuff rank badge on the side.

For summer and hot climates there was a white cap cover, single-breasted white tunic with stand collar, fly front, and white lace on the collar, front, skirt, pocket openings, and on the cuffs. It was worn with blue shoulder straps, long white trousers, and white canvas shoes. The white tunic for petty officers had open patch pockets. Ratings wore a white shirt, blue jumper with mid-blue collar edged with two white stripes, black scarf, and white cord knife lanyard, matching long trousers, and black leather boots or shoes. The hat had a blue or white top, and black silk ribbon with the name of the ship or installation, or in wartime *Regia Marina* in yellow or gold block letters. The summer uniform for ratings is illustrated in 133. Winter working dress is illustrated in 130. There was also a double-breasted peacoat with two rows of three brass buttons. Battle-dress was usually the same as working dress but with the addition of the steel helmet with yellow crowned foul anchor painted on the front, orange coloured life jacket with the rating's number painted on the front and back, and padded helmet for certain categories of rating.

When serving on land officers wore brown leather equipment, and ratings natural coloured or grey webbing of British manufacture (136), and grey-green puttees or grey webbing gaiters.

During the war in the tropics officers adopted khaki drill clothing as illustrated in 134.

Rank was indicated as follows:

Seamen	One narrow, or one medium, with one or two narrow red lace (black on khaki uniforms) inverted chevrons above, on both sleeves.
Petty officers (*Secondo capo and sergente*)	One medium with one or two narrow gold lace inverted chevrons on both upper sleeves.
Chief Petty Officers (*Capo*)	One to three gold lace stripes on the *passants*, and on the shoulder straps.
Lieutenants	One to three medium gold lace stripes with a curl on the only or uppermost, on the cuffs, and field cap. One to three medium gold lace rings on the peaked cap band. One to three five-pointed gold stars ensigned by a gold crown on the shoulder straps.
Captains	One wide with one to three medium gold lace

and Commanders	stripes with a curl on the uppermost, on the cuffs and field cap. One medium with one to three gold lace rings on the cap band. One to three five-pointed stars ensigned by a gold crown on the blue shoulder straps which were edged with gold.
Flag officers	Gold-embroidered *Greca* with one to four gold-embroidered stripes above, with a curl on the uppermost on the cuffs and field cap. Gold-embroidered *Greca* and one to four gold braid rings above on the peaked cap band. Gold lace shoulder straps with gold-embroidered crown above one to four five-pointed gold stars.

Only line officers were known by naval rank titles and wore the curl on the rank distinction lace; members of other corps used the following colours in the centre of the cap badge, as backing to the cap rings, cuff stripes, as piping on the shoulder straps and *passants*. Commissioned warrant officers (*Corpo Reale Equipaggi Marittimi*), had neither curl nor colour, but wore a gilt metal badge above their rank distinction lace on the cuffs and shoulder straps as follows:

Branch	Colour	Badge
Line	Uniform cloth	Foul anchor on shoulder straps.
Aides to flag officers	Uniform cloth	Five-pointed star inside curl.
Construction	Pink	Helmet on crossed hammer and axe.
Ordnance	Blue	Sword
Mechanical engineering	Blue	Propeller
Medicine	Turquoise	Geneva cross.
Pharmacists	Green	Aesculapius rod (no curl).
Commissary	Scarlet	Five-pointed star.
Port Captaincy	Grey-green	Foul anchor.
Chaplaincy	Purple	Gold cross.

Ratings wore their branch or trade badge above the rank chevrons. On the upper left sleeve at shoulder height, ratings wore one to four stripes which indicated the squadron. These stripes were in white on blue and red on white uniforms for members of the seamen branch, and red on blue, and blue on white uniforms for members of other branches.

Naval pilots and observers wore gilt metal wings, and crews of submarines, a circular gilt metal badge above the medal ribbons on the left breast.

After September 1943 various changes were made to the uniform of the navy of the Italian Social Republic. Briefly these were as follows: the crown on the cap badge was replaced by a winged bird, the five-pointed star on the ends of the collar was replaced by the *gladio*, lace rings on the cap band were abolished and instead lieutenants wore a blue and gold chin cord, and senior officers an all-gold one, the *passants* were simplified, and the traditional sailor's hat was replaced by a blue beret with a small yellow metal anchor on the front.

Marines

Marine officers wore army service dress [A.U. 39–42 and 46, 75] with naval cap badge, gold or yellow lace rank rings on the cap band and gold-embroidered *passants* on the shoulders. Other ranks wore a green beret with naval cap badges for n.c.o.s, and yellow metal anchor for other ranks, green version of the naval jumper, which could be worn with white shirt, blue jean collar, black scarf, and white knife lanyard, or more commonly with just a green polo-necked pullover (138). Members of the Nautical Parachute Battalion wore the parachutist's helmet.

In North Africa marines wore a light khaki drill beret, shirt, bush jacket (*sahariana*), pantaloons, long trousers, or shorts, with puttees, woollen stockings or webbing gaiters, and woollen stockings respectively, with ankle boots or shoes. There was also a khaki drill version of the jumper, with pointed cuffs and rectangular collar edged with two white stripes. In hot weather marines also wore their white uniforms as illustrated in 136. From 1943 onwards the grey green paratroop uniform (137) began to be issued to marines.

Officers wore naval rank badges, except that the rank distinction lace was worn on the outside of the cuff only, as in the army. In addition rank badges were worn on the left front of the beret, and towards the end of the war there was a tendency to move the rank badges from the cuffs to the shoulder straps. Other ranks wore the following badges of rank:

Other ranks	One wide with one or two narrow red (sometimes also black) lace inverted chevrons above, on the upper sleeves.
Petty Officers	One wide with two narrow gold lace inverted chevrons above on both upper sleeves.
Warrant Officers	One to three gold or yellow lace stripes across the shoulder straps.

All personnel wore scarlet collar or cuff patches with the lion of St Mark in gilt metal or yellow embroidery. The various arms within the regiment wore a distinguishing yellow metal badge above the rank chevrons.

After the armistice *San Marco* served with the *Folgore* Combat Group under allied command, and its personnel wore British battle-dress with a blue beret, on which existing insignia was worn. Officers wore pointed scarlet collar patches with the gilt St Mark lion and five-pointed star, and other ranks wore scarlet cuff patches with the lion embroidered in yellow. A *San Marco* division was also formed in the north, and trained in Germany, but although intended as a Marine division, it was in reality an infantry division, despite the traditional *San Marco* insignia being worn.

In the north an existing naval commando unit was expanded into a marine division *Decima Flottiglia MAS*. Its personnel wore the green uniform illustrated in 137. As in the navy the royal crown was replaced by a Germanified eagle with outstretched wings, and the five-pointed star by the white metal *gladio*. In addition all personnel wore a blue metal or cloth shield with a large roman ten above a gold death's head with a red rose in its mouth, and below *Flottiglia MAS* in gold letters. The red ten was also painted on the left side of the steel helmet until replaced by a white foul anchor on the front.

The following combination of colours and badges were worn on pointed collar patches:

Unit	Colour	Badge
Naval contingents incl. crews of surface and underwater vessels	White	Gold anchor and *gladio*.
Infantry battalions (to Feb. 1944*)	Brown	Lion and star.
Infantry battalions (to July 1944*)	Scarlet	Lion and *gladio*.
Infantry battalions (from July 1944*)	Blue	Lion and *gladio*.
Divisional Recce. Group	Black	Death's head and *gladio*.
Artillery and Btl. *Risoluti*	Yellow	*Gladio*.

Military police	Red/black	Lion and *gladio*.
Unassigned personnel and other land-based elements	Blue	Gold anchor and *gladio*.

*These colours also appeared in the centre of the cap badge. Other units wore dark blue cap badge centre.

ITALY   Royal and Republican Air Forces

The grey service uniform was introduced in 1923, and remained virtually unchanged until the end of the war, when there was an attempt to introduce a Germanified uniform in Mussolini's Italian Social Republic.

The basic service dress for officers and other ranks is illustrated in 140. Officers also wore matching grey breeches and black boots, side cap with rank badges on the left front, and double-breasted greatcoat with two rows of three gilt metal buttons, side pockets with flap and half-belt at the back. Rank distinction lace, *passants* and five-pointed stars (silver for officers and gold for generals) were worn on the greatcoat. The other ranks greatcoat was single-breasted with open collar and fly-front.

In hot weather or in the tropics officers wore the uniform illustrated in 142–43. The peaked cap with cover could also be worn with the white uniform, while during the war khaki drill uniforms and cap covers began to be worn.

Rank was indicated as follows:

Airmen	One wide with one or two narrow inverted red lace chevrons above, on the upper sleeves.
N.C.O.s	One wide with one or two narrow inverted gold lace chevrons above, on the upper sleeves. One or two narrow gold lace chevrons on the cape collar.
Warrant officers	One to three gold lace bars on the *passants* and shoulder straps. One gold lace bar on the side and field cap and beret, and one narrow gold lace ring on the cap band. One to three narrow gold lace chevrons on the cape collar.
Junior officers	One to three narrow gold lace stripes with a square loop on the only or uppermost, on the cuffs. One to three gold-embroidered five-pointed stars (1st lieutenant and 1st captain two and three stars respectively

with a narrow gold bar beneath) on the side and field cap and beret, woven band with one to three gold rings with blue between, on the cap band. Pointed grey cloth shoulder straps with one to three gold-embroidered five-pointed stars (1st lieutenant and 1st captain two and three stars respectively with a gold stripe across the base of the shoulder strap).

Senior officers   One medium with one to three narrow gold lace stripes above, with a square loop on the uppermost, on the cuffs. One to three five-pointed gold-embroidered stars on a rectangular grey cloth patch edged with gold, on the side and field cap and beret, and woven band with one medium and one to three narrow gold rings above, with blue between, on the cap band. Pointed grey cloth shoulder straps edged in gold, with one to three five-pointed gold-embroidered stars.

Generals   Gold-embroidered *greca* with one to four narrow gold-embroidered stripes above, with a square loop on the uppermost, on the cuffs, and in a reduced form on the side and field cap and beret. Gold-embroidered *greca* with one to four gold braid rings above on the cap band. Gold lace shoulder straps with one to three five-pointed silver-embroidered stars.

The various branches or *ruolo* were distinguished by the colour of the centre of the officer's cap badge, the design of the small circular gilt metal badge at the base of the cap badge wreath, by the colour of the backing to the rank distinction lace on the cuffs and cap band, as piping on the *passants* and shoulder straps and finally by the badge on the *passants* and shoulder straps as follows:

Branch	*Colour*	*Badge*
Generals	Crimson velvet	Sceptre on shoulder straps and *passants* and plain cap badge.
Aircrew	Blue	As for generals.
Services	Emerald green	Savoy Knot on shoulder straps and *passants* and cap badge.

Special services	Black	Four-bladed propeller super-imposed on M on shoulder straps, *passants* and cap badge
Engineering	Crimson velvet	Antique helmet on shoulder straps, *passants* and cap badge.
Technical assistance	Crimson	Antique helmet super-imposed on crossed axe and hammer on shoulder straps, *passants* and cap badge.
Administration	Black	Laurel wreath within circle on shoulder straps, *passants* and cap badge.
Commissariat	Scarlet	Open laurel wreath on shoulder straps, *passants* and cap badge.
Medical	Blue	Geneva cross on cap badge and Aesculapius on shoulder straps and *passants*.
Anti-aircraft artillery	Light blue then yellow from Sept. 1943	Crossed gun barrels on the shoulder straps and *passants*.

In addition pilots were distinguished by gilt metal wings worn above the medal ribbons, while aircrew warrant officers wore a winged bird on their *passants*, and other ranks on their shoulder straps.

With the establishment of the Italian Social Republic, air force uniform underwent certain changes. The crown on the cap badge and shoulder straps was replaced by a winged bird. The rank distinction rings on the cap band were abolished and instead officers wore German-pattern gold chin cords, and generals had gold-embroidery on the cap peak. *Passants* for officers and warrant officers were simplified, and new ones were introduced for anti-aircraft artillery. Finally the five-pointed star was replaced by the *gladio*. From September 1943 a series of white metal wings were adopted by aircrew for wear above the right breast pocket, but despite the fact that they were unofficial, they are still in use today.

During the latter stages of the war, a considerable number of Italian air force personnel underwent training with, or served alongside the *Luftwaffe*. They usually wore German Air Force uniform with German or Italian rank badges – or both, and the star of Savoy (later replaced by the *gladio*) on the ends of the collar on both sides, and a shield in the Italian national colours on the upper right sleeve.

Air Force Parachute Troops

Both the army and air force had parachute troops until September 1943, when the air force of the Italian Social Republic assumed command of all paratroop formations, with the exception of the naval Nautical Parachute Battalion.

Personnel of the air force parachute battalion *Arditi dell'Aria* wore the uniform illustrated in 148–50, and there was also a khaki drill version of this uniform.

In action parachutists wore the parachute pattern helmet [A.U. 219] with German or Italian camouflage pattern cover, smock made of Italian camouflage materials (148), or those of German manufacture (149), and camouflage or green trousers. Parachutes were of Italian manufacture.

Rank was indicated as in the other branches of the air force, except that rank badges were also sometimes worn on the left breast of the smock, and painted on the left side of the steel helmet.

The distinctive colour of parachute troops was light blue which appeared in the centre of the cap badge, and on the collar patches. Qualified parachutists wore a yellow silk or gold-embroidered falling parachute on the upper left sleeve [A.U. 129]. It was to have been replaced by an oval white metal badge for wear on the left breast, but it is doubtful if this badge was ever awarded.

JAPAN   Imperial Navy

The Japanese fleet came into existence at the end of the last century, and adopted the uniforms then in current use in the most important navies, which remained virtually unchanged until World War 2.

Officers wore a single-breasted blue tunic with stand collar and slash side pockets, and hook and eye fastening in front. The top and front edge of the collar, the front and skirt of the tunic, as well as the pockets were trimmed with black silk lace, which was also used to distinguish rank on the cuffs. During the war a simpler blue tunic (152) came into use.

The peaked cap is illustrated in 155, but during the war the most common form of head-dress was the peaked field cap as illustrated in 152.

The white summer uniform for officers is illustrated in 155. Petty officers wore a peaked cap with yellow metal cap badge, and single-breasted tunic with stand collar.

In winter sailors wore the basic dress as illustrated in 155, and for cold weather there was a double-breasted peacoat with two rows of five grey metal buttons and vertical slash side pockets. There were also many patterns of foul-weather and greatcoats, as well as a boat cape with stand collar.

In hot weather sailors wore a short-sleeved cotton shirt with blue edging around the neck opening, white cotton jumper with or without the blue jean collar, black scarf, and blue edging around the cuffs and skirt. For work or action sailors either wore the shirt on its own with white duck trousers, or the white duck working shirt (156), or a white working overall. Battle-dress normally included the steel helmet with anchor on the front, and life jacket.

During the war the most common form of tropical clothing was made of light khaki or olive drab drill as illustrated in 154.

Naval parachute troops wore a special olive drab uniform with army pattern parachute helmet [A.U. 110] with yellow anchor badge on the front, and special arm badge on the upper right sleeve. Fully qualified paratroopers wore a yellow silk embroidered winged badge on the right breast.

Rank was indicated by the collar patches on the blue and khaki tunics, and by the shoulder straps on the white tunic and blue greatcoat. Shoulder straps were also sometimes worn on the khaki tunic. On the blue field cap officers had yellow or gold, and on the white and khaki caps blue lace rings. On the cape collar the rank group was indicated by gold-embroidered cherry blossoms. From January 1944 a new system of rank badges was adopted for wear on the cuffs; it consisted of one to three narrow gold lace rings without curl, with one to three gold-embroidered cherry blossoms beneath. Collar patches and shoulder straps continued to be worn however.

Petty officers and seamen at first wore their rating and branch badge combined on the upper right sleeve, but during the war a new system was introduced. Thereafter the branch badge in red on blue or blue on white uniforms was worn on the right, while the rating badge in yellow was worn on the upper left sleeve.

Rank was indicated as follows:

Seamen	Branch badge, crossed branch badge, or crossed branch badge with cherry blossom above, all in red, and worn on upper right sleeve. Then yellow anchor with one to three horizontal yellow stripes above, all in yellow, and worn on upper left sleeve. All these badges were embroidered on cloth ground which corresponded to the colour of the uniform.
Petty officers	Branch badge, crossed branch badge, or crossed branch badge with cherry blossom above, inside an open wreath, all in red, and worn on upper right sleeve. Then anchor inside open wreath with one to three horizontal stripes above, all in yellow, and worn on upper left sleeve. All these badges were embroidered on a cloth ground which corresponded to the colour of the uniform.
Warrant officers	One medium gold lace bar on the collar patches and narrow gold lace stripe on the shoulder straps. Narrow black or gold lace ring with curl on the cuffs. One narrow lace ring on the field cap, and cuffs from January 1944.
Cadets	Yellow metal or gold-embroidered anchor on the collar, collar patches, and shoulder straps, and one narrow black or gold lace ring without curl on the cuffs, and one narrow lace ring on the field cap, and cuffs from January 1944.
Midshipmen	Yellow metal or gold-embroidered anchor on the collar or collar patches, and one medium gold lace stripe on the shoulder straps, and one narrow black or gold lace ring with curl on the cuffs, and one narrow lace ring on the field cap, and cuffs from January 1944.
Lieutenants	Medium gold lace stripe on collar patches and shoulder strap, with one to three silver cherry blossoms. One medium, one medium with one narrow beneath, or one medium with two narrow lace rings beneath, with a curl on the only or uppermost on the cuffs. One medium lace ring on the field cap, and one medium lace ring with one to three cherry blossoms beneath,

on the cuffs from January 1944. One cherry blossom on the cape collar.

Captains and Commanders	Two medium gold lace stripes on the collar patches and shoulder straps, with one to three silver cherry blossoms. Two medium with one narrow beneath, and three or four medium lace stripes, with a curl on the uppermost on the cuffs. Two medium lace rings on the field cap, and two medium lace rings with one to three cherry blossoms beneath, on the cuffs from January 1944. Two cherry blossoms on the cape collar.
Flag officers	One wide gold lace stripe on the collar patches and shoulder straps, with one to three silver cherry blossoms. Two wide, with one to three medium lace rings with a curl on the uppermost on the cuffs. Three medium lace rings on the field cap, and three medium lace rings with one to three cherry blossoms beneath, on the cuffs from January 1944. Three cherry blossoms on the cape collar.

Officers commissioned from the ranks could rise to rank of lieutenant, and were distinguished from regular officers by having narrower lace on the collar patches and shoulder straps. Ensigns had three cherry blossoms in place of the ring, while lieutenants had three cherry blossoms under their rank distinction lace. Reserve officers up to the rank of captain wore the same number and width of rank distinction lace, but in the shape of a chevron on the cuffs, and their cap badge, instead of being all gold, was embroidered in gold and silver.

Corps colours appeared as piping on the collar patches and shoulder straps, and as piping on the bottom edge of the peaked cap band. The anchor in the centre of the cap badge for midshipmen and cadets was also in the corps colour. For petty officers and ratings the cherry blossom between the anchor and stripes (on the final pattern badges) was in the corps colour, which were basically as follows:

Corps	*Colour*
Ship and engine constructors	Brown
Ordnance constructors	Purple brown
Hydrographers	Light blue
Survey officers	Black
Paymasters	White

Surgeons	Scarlet
Engineers	Violet
Justice	Pale green
Chief carpenter (warrant officer)	Green
Bandmaster (warrant officer)	Grey-blue

JAPAN   Air Force

Since the air force formed part of the army, its personnel wore army uniforms and badges of rank [A.U. pp. 42–45 and 87, 115 & 200].

THE NETHERLANDS   Royal Navy

The Dutch navy came into existence at the end of the sixteenth century. Although defeated in May 1940, naval forces continued to fight in the Pacific, and contingents served alongside the British Royal Navy. Dutch naval uniform as worn during the war was the result of the Royal Decree of 26 September 1932, which came into force on 1 April 1933.

The basic uniform for officers and ratings is illustrated in 164 and 163. Officers did not have a greatcoat as such, but wore a double-breasted frock coat with *passants* and two rows of six buttons, and rank distinction lace on the cuffs. Ratings were issued with a double-breasted peacoat which was worn with the blue jean collar outside. During the war the cap tally with *Koninklijke Marine* was changed from Gothic to block script.

For summer wear there was a white cap cover, white jumper with blue jean collar, white trousers and black leather shoes. The white jumper was worn outside the white trousers, but the blue jumper was worn inside, with black leather waistbelt with brass buckle.

In the tropics ratings wore either a white sun helmet or straw panama hat with cap tally, short-sleeved shirt with blue jean edging around the neck opening and sleeves, white belt with brass buckle, white shorts and socks and black leather shoes. Officers wore the normal white collar-attached shirt, and white shoes.

Rank was indicated as follows for executive officers, while those in non-combatant civil branches wore white or silver rank badges:

Seamen	Red anchor for 2nd class, and crossed red anchors for 1st class seaman. Leading seaman in seaman branch was known as a *Kwartier-meester* and wore one yellow anchor on the upper left sleeve of the jumper and wide yellow chevron on the cuffs of the peacoat. Leading seamen in other branches were known as *Korporaal* and wore a yellow tape chevron on both upper sleeves of the jumper, and wide yellow chevron on the cuffs of the peacoat.
Petty and chief petty officers	Square dark blue collar patches edged with one or two rows of narrow gold lace on the front and bottom edges only, on the white and grey-green tunic. On the blue jacket they wore one or two gold lace chevrons on both cuffs.
Cadets	One gold lace chevron on both cuffs.
Warrant officers	One narrow gold lace ring with curl on the cuffs and shoulder straps.
Lieutenants	One, two, or two medium with one narrow 'half' ring between, with a curl on the only or uppermost, on the cuffs and shoulder straps.
Captains and Commanders	Three or four medium gold lace rings with a curl on the uppermost on the cuffs and shoulder straps. One row of gold oak leaves on the cap peak.
Flag officers	One wide with one medium gold lace ring above with a curl, and two to four six-pointed silver stars above, on the cuffs and shoulder straps. Cap peak embroidered all round with gold oak leaves.

On the ends of the cape collar all officers wore the same number and size of stripes and stars, as on the cuffs and shoulder straps, but in a smaller embroidered version.

Officers in the various branches were distinguished as follows:

Corps	*Collar/cap badge*	*Badges/buttons*
Line	Foul anchor	Gold
Aviation	Radial motor and propeller	Gold

Engineering	Crossed arrows and torch	Gold
Administration	Foul anchor in silver	Silver
Special Service	Corps badge and SD in curl	Gold

Naval aircrew wore the following gilt metal or gold-embroidered wings on the left breast:

Pilot	Gilt metal winged bird superimposed on orange enamel sun.
Pilot observer	Gilt metal winged bird superimposed on orange enamel sun, ensigning a blue enamel circle charged with letter 'w'.
Observer	Blue enamel circle charged with letter 'w' and one gilt metal wing.
Air telegraphist gunner	Blue enamel circle charged with letters 'T', 'M', and 's' and one gilt metal wing.
Air gunner	Blue enamel circle charged with letters 'M' and 's' and one gilt metal wing.
Air telegraphist	Blue enamel circle charged with letter 'T'.

During the war Dutch personnel serving with the Royal Navy wore the shoulder flash 'Holland', and sometimes their national colours on the hat or painted on the side of the British steel helmet.

Royal Marine Corps

The Marine Corps was originally formed in 1665, and by the beginning of World War 2 comprised some 1,500 men. After the German invasion marines continued to fight against the Japanese, while others formed a battle group in the *Prinses Irene Brigade*. In 1944 the U.S. Marine Corps trained a further 4,500 Dutch marines, who were eventually formed into a brigade. As a result Dutch marines wore Dutch, British, and American uniforms.

The blue service dress for other ranks is illustrated in 167, while that of officers was basically the same except that it was open and worn with white shirt and black tie, and had a matching cloth belt with gilt metal buckle. Shoes were black and gloves and waistbelt brown leather.

The grey-green service dress (168) was similar to that of the Dutch army [A.U. pp. 45–47 and 29–30], while the tropical version is illustrated in 169. Additional items were the black painted M.1928 steel helmet [A.U. 217] with silvered metal crowned foul anchor on the front, grey-green side cap and peaked cap, and blue marine-pattern greatcoat with brass buttons.

Marine personnel serving in England wore battle-dress with curved khaki shoulder flash edged in dark red with *Nederlands Marines* in dark red, above the gold star emblem of the Marine Corps on a blue ground, with beneath it a straight flash with *Korps Mariniers* in dark red on khaki.

Marines trained and equipped in the United States wore U.S. Marine uniform with Dutch Marine cap and collar badges. On U.S. combat clothing the Dutch marine emblem was printed in black on the left breast pocket (166).

Rank was indicated as follows:

Dutch uniform	Officers wore naval rank distinction lace on blue cloth slides on the shoulder straps, and petty officers wore square blue collar patches edged with gold lace, as prescribed for the white tunic.
British uniform	As on Dutch uniform.
U.S.M.C. uniform	Naval rank distinction lace on the shoulder straps of service dress. On combat dress either U.S.M.C. rank badges or reduced version of Dutch naval rank badges in brass worn on the ends of the collar on both sides.

THE NETHERLANDS   Military Air Force

Since the air force formed part of the army, its 600 men wore army uniforms [A.U. pp. 45–47 and 29–30] with light blue piping. Officers wore gold-embroidered rotary engine and propeller badge on both sides of the collar, and other ranks wore the same badge in bronzed metal. Pilots wore gilt metal wings above the left breast pocket of the tunic, and in the corresponding position on the greatcoat.

Flying clothing is believed to have been of French manufacture and included the black leather jacket illustrated in 31.

In June 1940 a unit of the Royal Dutch Naval Air Service became No. 320 (Dutch) Squadron R.A.F. At first its personnel continued to wear Dutch naval uniform, but later R.A.F. uniforms were issued. The

Dutch lion in gilt metal for officers and bronzed metal for other ranks was worn on the left front of the side cap, and the shoulder flash *Nederland* on the sleeves at shoulder height.

Dutch East Indies Military Air Force

According to the regulations of 1939 air force personnel were to wear either a white full or undress uniform with detachable collar patches which indicated rank, and stiff shoulder straps, or a light yellowish khaki drill service uniform.

The peaked cap was light khaki with black cloth band, and black leather peak and chin strap. On the front all ranks wore a circular orange cockade. The single-breasted open tunic had pleated patch breast, and patch side pockets with pointed flap and button, matching cloth belt, and pointed cuffs. It was worn with light khaki short-sleeved shirt, black tie, matching breeches or long trousers with black leather boots or shoes respectively. There was also a side cap with black leather chin strap.

On the light khaki flying suit, shirt, overalls and sports clothes rank was indicated by white or yellow metal badges on black cloth triangles, which were worn on the shoulder straps as follows:

1st class corporals	One large yellow metal hexagon and one vertical white metal bar.
Sergeants (Europeans)	One small yellow metal hexagon and one vertical white metal bar.
Adjutants	One white metal ball button.
Ensigns	One gold and one silver ball button.
Company officers	Two silver ball buttons, or one to three six-pointed silver stars.
Field officers	One gold bar with one to three six-pointed silver stars above.

On the right breast flying personnel wore the following wings:

Pilot	Bronzed metal winged bird.
Observer	Bronzed metal winged oak wreath with 'w' in the centre.
Pilot observer	Bronzed metal winged bird holding an oak wreath with 'w' in the centre, in its talons.
Flying doctor	Bronzed metal winged laurel wreath with rod of Aesculapius in the centre.

After the fall of Singapore some Dutch pilots escaped to Australia where they formed the nucleus of a Netherlands East Indies squadron.

NORWAY
Royal Navy

Naval uniform as worn during World War 2 was based on regulations issued in October 1907.

The standard service dress for officers and chief petty officers is illustrated in 171. The greatcoat was double-breasted. The blue peaked cap had black leather peak and chin strap, and gold-embroidered cap badge for petty officers, officers, and flag officers.

Ratings wore a white shirt with neck opening edged in mid-blue jean, blue jumper with blue jean collar edged with three white stripes, and a black scarf. Trousers were made of matching material. In summer ratings wore a white version of the blue uniform, and in winter they wore a blue peacoat with the blue jean collar on the outside. The hat was blue with blue pompom on the top, and black ribbon with *Den Kgl. Norske Marine* in yellow or gold lettering. Above the ribbon on the front was a circular metal cockade in the national colours – red, white, and blue.

Seamen	Crowned red foul anchor, or crowned red foul anchor above one or two diagonal red lace stripes on the upper left sleeve.
Junior petty officers	One red lace chevron on both cuffs.
Senior petty officers	One gold lace chevron on both cuffs.
Chief petty officers	Two gold lace chevrons on both cuffs.
Cadets	One to three (class 1 to 3) five-pointed gold metal stars on both cuffs.
Lieutenants	One to four gold lace rings one with a curl on the only or uppermost on the cuffs and shoulder straps. During the war the rank of Lieutenant Commander with five rings was introduced.
Commodores	One medium with three narrow gold lace rings above, with a curl on the uppermost, on the cuffs and shoulder straps.
Flag officers	One wide gold lace ring, with one narrow beneath, and one to three narrow gold lace rings above, with a curl on the uppermost, on the cuffs. Gold

lace shoulder straps with one to three silver five-pointed stars.

The corps or branch was indicated as follows:

Branch	Distinction
Royal Naval Reserve	No curl.
Royal Naval Volunteer Reserve	Elongated curl.
Engineering officers	Curl replaced by triple bladed ship's propeller.
Medical officers	No curl and scarlet piping on top edge of uppermost ring.
Administrative officers	No curl and light blue piping.
Paymasters	No curl and white piping.
Engineers	Purple piping.
Constructors	Grey piping.

Ratings wore their branch badges as follows:

Rate	Badge colour	Position
Seamen	Red	Upper left sleeve.
Petty officers	Red	Above rings on cuff.
Chief petty officers	Gold	Upper left sleeve.

Norwegian personnel serving with the Royal Navy continued to wear their old uniforms, or those of the Royal Navy, but with the Norwegian flag on the upper right and either 'Norge' or 'Norway' on the upper left sleeve at shoulder height.

Norway Army Aviation (Air Force)

Since its formation in 1912 the air service formed part of the army, and its personnel wore army uniforms [A.U. pp. 47–48 and 17–18] with light green piping. In the spring of 1940 plans for the re-organisation and re-equipping of the army and naval air services began to be put into effect. Following the German invasion Norwegian personnel escaped to England where they served with the R.A.F., while others underwent training in Canada. In 1941 the Norwegian Air Force became a separate arm with its own grey uniforms (121) and rank badges based on the British pattern.

From 1941 rank was indicated as follows:

N.C.O.s	One to three blue chevrons on both upper sleeves, and on the greatcoat shoulder straps. Flight Sergeant three blue chevrons with the Norwegian coat of arms in bronzed metal underneath.
Junior officers	One to three five-pointed white metal or silver-embroidered stars on the ends of the collar of the tunic and battle-dress blouse, and on the greatcoat shoulder straps.
Senior officers	Silver lace on the front and bottom edge of the tunic and battle-dress blouse collar, and one to three five-pointed white metal or silver-embroidered stars. The greatcoat shoulder straps were edged with silver lace and had one to three stars as above. Silver chin cords on the peaked cap.
Generals	Wide gold lace on the front and bottom edges of the tunic and battle-dress blouse collar, and one to three five-pointed white metal or silver-embroidered stars. The greatcoat shoulder straps were made of gold lace with one to three five-pointed stars. Gold cords on the peaked cap.

Qualified aircrew such as pilots, observers and wireless operators/air gunners wore embroidered wings above the right breast pocket.

POLAND   Navy

The navy was established soon after the country gained independence after World War 1, but it was not until 1929 that a fleet as such really began to take shape. Uniform worn during the war was the result of regulations issued in 1920 and amended in 1922, 1927, and 1930.

Naval officers, warrant officers and chief petty officers all wore the same basic uniform as illustrated in 173. The greatcoat was double-breasted with two rows of four gilt buttons. In hot weather they wore a white cap cover, single-breasted white tunic with stand collar, four buttons, matching long white trousers and white canvas shoes.

Cadets wore the same uniform as chief petty officers but with gilt metal 'SP' or 'SPR' (reserve) badge on the ends of the collar on both sides.

These badges also appeared on the shoulder straps of the white tunic, which were piped in red and white twisted cord for reserve cadets.

Seamen and junior n.c.o.s wore the uniform illustrated in 174. In cold weather they also wore a double-breasted peacoat, which was also worn by petty officers, chief petty officers, warrant officers, cadets, and officers with rank badges on the cuffs or sleeve, but shoulder straps were not permitted.

In the summer or in the tropics ratings wore the white uniform (172). During the war they also wore British naval tropical dress. Working dress included a white American pattern hat, and white denim jumper and trousers. Petty officers wore a blue single-breasted tunic with stand collar, patch pockets and five buttons in front.

Rank distinction lace appeared on the cuffs and shoulder straps for officers, warrant officers and petty officers, and on the upper left sleeve for other ratings. In addition officers had gold braid on the cap peak according to rank group, and five-pointed stars on the chin strap indicating exact rank. Petty officers had a special cap badge.

Rank was indicated as follows:

Seamen	One or two diagonal gold lace stripes edged in red on the upper left sleeve.
Petty officers	Three diagonal gold lace stripes edged in red on the upper left sleeve.
Chief petty officers	One or two inverted gold lace chevrons edged in red on the cuffs and shoulder straps. Until April 1942 chief petty officers wore a narrow gold lace ring under the two inverted chevrons, but during the war he was classed as a warrant officer and wore one narrow gold lace ring with curl and officers cap badge.
Cadets	Badges as for petty officers with an additional narrow gold lace ring for each year of training (one to three years). During the war only the gold lace rings were retained on the cuffs only. Cap badge as for petty officers.
Captains (junior officers)	One to three gold lace rings with a curl on the only or uppermost on the cuffs and shoulder straps. One row of gold braid on the cap peak, and one to three five-pointed white metal stars on the chin strap.

Commanders (senior officers)	One medium with one to three narrow gold lace rings above with a curl on the uppermost, on the cuffs and shoulder straps. Two rows of gold braid on the cap peak and one to three five-pointed white metal stars on the chin strap.
Admirals	Gold lace zigzag with one to three narrow gold lace rings with a curl on the uppermost, on the cuffs and shoulder straps. Gold zigzag on the cap peak and one to three five-pointed white metal stars on the chin strap.

Before the war rank distinction lace went right round the cuff, but from 1941 on it was sewn on the outside only for economy reasons.

From 30 November 1938 corps or branch colours appeared as backing or 'lights' to the rank distinction lace as follows:

Branch	Colour
Engineering	Scarlet
Coastal and rivers	Cornflower blue
Technical services	Emerald green
Administration	White (brown from March 1944)
Medical	Raspberry
Administration	White
Army intendance officers attached to the navy	Brown
Commissary	White

Trade and speciality badges were worn on the upper left sleeve in yellow for petty officers and red for seamen.

During the war Polish naval personnel serving with the Royal Navy continued to wear Polish uniform, although minor modifications were made to bring it more in line with that of the Royal Navy. For example in October 1941 officers, warrant officers, officer cadets, and chief petty officers, were permitted to wear the blue gabardine raincoat, and the same shoulder straps on the peacoat as on the greatcoat. Blue battle-dress and other kinds of British tropical, working, and foul weather clothing were also made available.

Military Aviation and Polish Air Force (P.A.F.)

From its formation until 1936 Military Aviation personnel wore army uniforms [A.U. pp. 49–50] with yellow collar patches and cap bands, and white metal or cloth wings on the upper left sleeve of the tunic and greatcoat. In 1936 a new 'steel blue' or grey uniform was introduced, which was to have been adopted by officers and regular non-commissioned officers not later than 1 April 1938.

The grey service dress for officers is illustrated in 176. Generals had silver-embroidered Polish eagle on the ends of the collar on both sides, silver-embroidered zigzag around both cuffs, and black *lampassen* on trousers and breeches. Staff officers had the Polish eagle in white metal on the collar, and reserve officers the letters 's.p.r.' within a wreath. Regular cadets wore black cloth shoulder straps and white metal sword and oak-leaves on the collar. Medical and administrative officers wore cherry or royal blue cloth backing to the braid on the cap peak, and as lace on the trousers and cuffs respectively.

The greatcoat was grey and double-breasted with two rows of three white metal buttons, matching shoulder straps, turn-back cuffs, and half-belt fastened at the back with two buttons. Generals, staff officers and officer cadets wore the same badges on the greatcoat as on the tunic collar. There was also a black leather double-breasted coat with black cloth collar and shoulder straps, which were to be worn plain without rank badges, but this order appears to have often been ignored.

The other ranks grey tunic was single-breasted with stand-and-fall collar matching shoulder straps, seven white metal buttons in front, breast and side patch pockets with straight flap and button, and straight cuffs fastened at the back with one button. The tunic was worn with matching pantaloons, puttees and ankle boots, or long trousers and black shoes.

Lance-corporal	One silver lace stripe across the shoulder strap, and on the front of the peaked cap, and left front of the beret.
N.C.O.s	Two to three silver lace stripes or one or two inverted silver lace chevrons across the shoulder straps which were edged in silver lace. Stripes and chevrons were

	also worn on the front of the peaked cap, and left front of the beret.
Warrant officers	One five-pointed silver star on the shoulder straps which were edged with silver lace. Silver star on the front, and red braid around the top of the cap band. Silver star above red braid stripe on the left front of the beret, and in the centre of a circular black cloth badge on the upper left sleeve of the flying suit.
Junior officers	One to three five-pointed silver stars on the shoulder straps, and on the front of the cap, and on the left front of the beret. Circular black cloth badge edged with silver braid, with one to three five-pointed silver stars in the centre, on the upper left sleeve of the flying suit. One row of silver braid on the cap peak.
Senior officers	One to three five-pointed silver stars above two silver stripes on the shoulder straps and on the left front of the beret. One to three five-pointed silver stars, and two rows of silver braid on the cap peak. Circular black cloth badge edged with silver braid, and with one to three five-pointed silver stars above two silver-embroidered bars in the centre, on the upper left sleeve of the flying suit.
General officers	Silver-embroidered zigzag and one to three five-pointed silver stars above, on the shoulder straps, and on the left front of the beret. One to three five-pointed stars on the front of the cap, and silver embroidered zigzag on the cap peak. Circular black cloth badge edged in silver braid with one to three five-pointed silver stars above a silver embroidered zigzag in the centre, on the upper left sleeve of the flying suit.

Flying personnel wore a white or gilt metal diving eagle suspended from a small chain above the left breast pocket. The various categories wore a distinguishing letter in white or gilt metal in the centre of the wreath held in the eagle's beak. Squadron, or badges of former army regiments were worn on the left breast pocket, or painted on the front of the life jacket.

In January 1940 it was agreed that Poles would serve first in the French Air Force, and then in independent Polish formations. They were to wear French uniforms with Polish cap and rank badges (31). From December

1939 Polish personnel also began to serve with the British Royal Air Force Volunteer Reserve, and in August 1940 an independent Polish Air Force (P.A.F.) was established in England.

It was originally intended that all foreign personnel serving in the R.A.F. would belong to the Volunteer Reserve, and wear British uniform with national shoulder flashes, but the establishment of the Polish Air Force meant that Poles began to wear their own cap badge, and Polish air force rank in the form of collar patches, and their acting R.A.F. rank in the normal British manner. In order to conform to R.A.F. practice all Polish air force badges were changed from silver to gold, except the other ranks cap eagle which remained in white metal. The officers cap badge, which was formerly embroidered in silver, was manufactured with silver eagle, and gold feathered wings and shield. The 'Poland' shoulder flash was embroidered in gold for officers or light blue for other ranks on grey or dark blue ground. There was also a shoulder flash for Polish volunteers from countries other than Poland. According to regulations Polish warrant officers and flight sergeants in the Polish Air Force wore a large button on light blue and black cloth discs and small button only, respectively, but in practice Polish personnel also wore the corresponding R.A.F. rank badges. Polish Air Force personnel also served alongside the Red Army on the Eastern Front, and wore any remaining items of old Polish, or Soviet Russian air force uniform with Polish rank badges on the shoulder straps and white or silver lace stripes on the cuffs (e.g. a captain wore three stars on the shoulder straps, and four stripes on the cuffs).

RUMANIA   Royal Navy

Rumanian naval officers began to wear blue in the middle of the last century, when they adopted a French-style uniform. Between the wars the uniform developed along British lines. The uniform worn during World War 2 was introduced in May 1921.

Officers uniform is illustrated in 179. The greatcoat was double-breasted with two rows of four gilt metal buttons. Unlike most navies, officers wore rank distinction lace on the greatcoat cuffs. The white tunic was single-breasted with stand collar and blue shoulder straps, five gilt metal buttons, patch breast and side pockets with straight flap and button. It was worn with white cap cover, white trousers and white canvas shoes.

Petty officers (Masters) wore a single-breasted blue tunic with stand collar and five gilt metal buttons, slash left breast pocket, and side pockets with straight flaps, matching long trousers, and black shoes. The peaked cap was blue with black peak and chin strap and yellow metal anchor badge.

Ratings wore a blue and white striped shirt, blue jumper worn outside the trousers, blue jean collar edged with three white stripes, and black scarf. The hat was the German pattern with '*Marina Regala*' in yellow on the ribbon which was worn without the long ribbon hanging at the back.

Rank was indicated as follows:

Seamen	One to three red tape stripes under the trade or speciality badge on the upper left sleeve.
Petty officers	One or two narrow, or one medium and one narrow gold lace stripes under the trade or speciality badge on the upper left sleeve.
Cadets	Four gilt metal buttons on the cuffs.
Midshipmen	One narrow gold lace ring with curl on the cuffs and shoulder straps.
Lieutenants	Two or three narrow gold lace rings with curl on the uppermost, on the cuffs and shoulder straps.
Captains and Commanders	One medium, with one to three narrow gold lace rings with a curl on the uppermost above, on the cuffs and shoulder straps. One row of gold-embroidered oak leaves on the cap peak.
Flag officers	Two wide, with one or two medium gold lace rings above with a curl on the uppermost, on the cuffs and shoulder straps. Two rows of gold-embroidered oak leaves on the cap peak.

The following corps were identified by coloured backing or 'lights' to the rank distinction lace:

Corps	Colour
Engineers	Purple
Supply	Silver rank distinction lace
Doctors	Crimson
Naval construction	Light blue
Pharmacists	Green
Band	Grey

Naval aviators wore a foul anchor on the ends of the jacket collar on both sides. Towards the end of the war gilt metal war badges, based on the German model were introduced for wear by personnel in the various branches (submarines, cruisers, minesweepers etc.) who had been in action.

RUMANIA   Royal Air Force

In 1931 the Rumanian Air Force changed its khaki uniforms for grey ones which were similar to those of the R.A.F. By 1939 the air force had grown to some 45,000 men and 1,000 machines. Officers wore a single-breasted open grey tunic with four gilt metal buttons, pleated patch breast, and side pockets with three-pointed flap and button, matching cloth belt with gilt metal buckle, and two small buttons on the outside of the cuff at the back. The shirt was grey or white, the tie black, and matching long trousers or breeches, with light blue *lampassen* for generals, were worn with black leather shoes or boots. The greatcoat was double-breasted with large pointed fall collar, turn-back cuffs, and side pockets with straight flaps.

The peaked cap was grey with dark blue mohair band, black leather peak, embroidered with gold oak leaves for senior officers, and black leather chin strap edged with gold wire. The cap badge was embroidered in gold for officers and made of yellow metal for other ranks. In addition to the side cap (178), all ranks wore a dark blue beret with badge on the left side. In hot weather officers wore a white cap cover and white tunic with rank badges on grey shoulder straps. The waistbelt and cross strap was brown leather, and with undress uniform officers wore a gilt metal dagger with white plastic grip. At first other ranks wore a grey version of the army uniform, but during the war a new battle dress-type field and working uniform was introduced. The blouse was single-breasted with stand-and-fall collar, matching shoulder straps, and five buttons in front. The patch breast pockets had a flap and button, and the long trousers had diagonal slash side pockets, and were worn gathered at the ankle like ski trousers. Footwear was brown leather, and there were also canvas anklets.

During the war the air force relied on Germany for much of its heavy equipment and aircraft, and even flying clothing.

Rank was indicated by gold lace on the cuffs of the tunic, and on the upper left sleeve of the greatcoat, and on grey shoulder straps on the white tunic. Other ranks wore their rank badges on the shoulder straps. On flying clothing rank badges were worn in many different places, for example on the front of the side cap below the badge, on the shoulders or shoulder straps (178), or above the left breast pocket of working overalls, flying suit, or jacket.

Regulation rank badges were as follows:

Corporals	One or two narrow yellow lace stripes on grey shoulder straps.
N.C.O.s (ground crew)	One to four narrow gold lace chevrons on grey shoulder straps with gold piping.
N.C.O.s (aircrew)	One to four yellow metal wings on grey shoulder straps with gold piping.
Junior officers	One to three narrow gold lace stripes with a rhomboid on the only or uppermost stripe, on the cuffs, greatcoat sleeve, and shoulder straps.
Senior officers	One medium with one to three narrow gold lace stripes above, with a rhomboid on the uppermost, on the cuffs, greatcoat sleeve, and shoulder straps.
General officers	One wide, with one medium above, and one or two narrow gold lace stripes above that, with a rhomboid on the uppermost stripe, on the cuffs, greatcoat sleeve and shoulder straps. Two rows of gold oak leaves on the cap peak, and light blue pointed collar patches with gold embroidery, and light blue *lampassen* on the trousers and breeches.

The following branches of the air force were distinguished by coloured collar patches, and coloured backing to the cuff stripes as follows:

Branch	Colour
Generals	Light blue
General staff	Dark blue
Fighters	Dark green
Bombers	Scarlet
Reconnaissance/Parachute troops	Light blue
Anti-aircraft artillery	Black
Engineers	Bright blue

178

Aerostation	Brown
Schools	Orange
Mechanics	Violet
Doctors	Crimson

In addition white metal badges were worn above the left breast pocket by fighter and bomber pilots, and observers. Members of the sea plane flotilla wore collar patches in the above colours, but with the addition of a yellow metal anchor.

SLOVAKIA   Air Force

Before the war Slovakia had formed part of Czechoslovakia, but in March 1939 it became a semi-independent protectorate of Germany. Slovak personnel who had served in the former Czech Air Force continued to wear Czech army khaki service, or dark blue undress uniform with new cap badges and rank distinctions.

The khaki service dress for officers is illustrated in 180. The greatcoat was double-breasted with two rows of five gilt metal buttons, slanting side pockets with flap, half-belt with three buttons, and khaki velvet collar.

In addition to the peaked cap there was a side cap with piping around the cuff, and shield-shaped national emblem in gilt for officers, white for n.c.o.s, and bronzed metal for other ranks.

The grey service dress originally introduced in 1938 for the Czech air force, was basically the same as the khaki one, except that it had matching pointed shoulder straps piped in gold for officers and silver for n.c.o.s. It was worn with white shirt, black tie, matching long trousers or breeches and black leather footwear. Trousers were piped for n.c.o.s, had a stripe for officers, and *lampassen* for generals. The grey peaked cap had a black leather peak.

The summer flying suit was made of beige canvas with zip-fasteners and thigh pockets, while the winter suit was made of leather with fur lining. As the war progressed the Germans supplied machines and equipment in increasing quantities.

The rank group was indicated by the button colour which was gilt for officers, silver for n.c.o.s, and bronze for other ranks. Rank badges were worn on the collar, and on the front of the flying suit as follows:

Airmen	One or two five-pointed white metal stars on the collar patches.
N.C.O.s	One to three five-pointed white metal stars on red and silver horizontally striped collar patches. Same patches were also worn on the front of the flying suit.
Company officers	One to three five-pointed gold-embroidered stars on gold-piped collar patches. Same distinctions worn on rectangular patch on the front of the flying suit.
Field officers	One to three five-pointed gold-embroidered stars above a line or gold-embroidery on gold-piped collar patches. Same distinctions were worn on a rectangular patch on the front of the flying suit.
Generals	Gold-embroidered collar patches with one or two five-pointed silver-embroidered stars. Cap peak embroidered with gold lime leaves.

Branch colours appeared as piping on the head-dress, collar patches on both khaki and grey tunics and greatcoat, and as stripe and piping on the long grey trousers. All air force personnel wore light blue except general officers and anti-aircraft artillery who wore scarlet.

Flying badges were worn on the left breast pocket as follows:

Pilots of former Czech Air Force	Gilt winged silver sword on matt silver wreath. Worn on right breast pocket.
Night fighter pilots	Gilt metal eagle and wreath.
Fighter pilots	Gilt metal eagle and silver wreath.
Air gunner/Army pilots	Silver eagle and wreath.
Night observer	Silver eagle and gilt wreath.
Technical personnel	Silver triple-bladed propeller on gold wreath.

UNITED STATES OF AMERICA   United States Navy

The basic naval uniform of World War 2 was a development of that originally introduced in 1862, and modified on numerous occasions thereafter. In 1941 uniform was once again reviewed and standardised. Officers and chief petty officers wore the uniform illustrated in 183, and the greatcoat in 182. There was also a double-breasted blue raincoat with two rows of four plain flat black plastic buttons, and matching belt, and it was worn without badges.

Peaked caps were worn with different coloured covers according to the season or order of dress. In 1943, a side or 'garrison' cap in blue with army pattern rank badges on the right, and naval badge on the left, was introduced for officers.

The white service uniform is illustrated in 188, but during the war the light khaki uniform (187) was more popular, although attempts were made to improve its protective colouring by dyeing it grey. On the grey uniform, buttons, and rank distinction lace on the grey shoulder straps, were black. Shirt-sleeve order consisted of khaki drill shirt, which was worn open or closed with black tie, and slightly smaller version of the army rank badges on the ends of the collar on both sides, matching long trousers, black socks, and black leather shoes.

There was also a khaki drill version of the side cap.

The basic blue uniform with dress jumper is illustrated in 184, and the peacoat and working hat in 185. The undress jumper had a plain matching collar and straight cuffs.

Some of the most typical working clothing is illustrated in 190–92.

Flight deck personnel on aircraft carriers adopted coloured helmets, baseball caps, T-shirts and jackets with their name, rank and function painted in black on the front and back (195). During the war these colours did not become standardised throughout the navy, and different colours were used on other carriers, but the following colours were typical:

Function	Colour
Plane captains	Brown
Plane handlers	Grey
Fire detail	Red
Firemen	Red
Arresting gear detail	Green
Hangarmen	Yellow
Ordnance men	Pink

On the battleship *Iowa* damage control men wore red helmets.

Naval aviators wore the green working uniform as illustrated in 194, and which included an overcoat in civilian cut with two rows of three large flat plastic buttons. All other items of clothing and orders of dress were as for naval officers. Gilt metal aviation qualification devices or 'wings' were worn above the left breast pocket.

Officers and warrant officers rank was indicated by lace rings on the cuffs and shoulder straps, slightly smaller version of army rank badges on both sides of the shirt collar for executive, and on the right side only for other officers, as well as on the left front of the side cap. Petty officers wore a special cap badge and their rank badges on the upper right (executive) or left (other branches) sleeve. Ratings wore white stripes on the cuffs of blue dress jumper.

The colour of rank badges changed according to the colour of the uniform on which they were worn:

Uniform colour	Colour
Blue	Gold or red
Blue shoulder straps	Gold
Grey and green working uniforms	Black
Blue greatcoat cuffs	Black
Petty officers grey, khaki and white uniforms	Blue
Ratings white uniforms	Blue

Rank was indicated as follows:

Seamen	One or two white stripes on the cuffs of the blue dress jumper. In wartime jumpers with one stripe were discontinued.
Petty officers	Three white stripes on the cuffs and one to three inverted chevrons ensigned by an eagle on the upper left or right sleeve. Petty officers with more than twelve years service wore gold chevrons on the blue jacket.
Chief petty officers	Three inverted chevrons, the top one joined by an arc, ensigned by an eagle on the upper left or right sleeve. Chief petty officers with more than twelve years service wore gold chevrons on the blue jacket, and had a special cap badge.
Warrant officers	One narrow gold and blue lace ring on the cuffs and shoulder straps, and bevelled gilt metal bar with 1/16 in. wide blue enamel stripe across the centre, on the shirt collar and side cap.
Chief warrant officer	One medium gold and blue lace ring on the cuffs

	and shoulder straps and flat gilt metal bar with 1/8 in. wide blue enamel stripe across the centre, on the shirt collar and side cap.
Ensign	One medium gold lace ring on the cuffs and shoulder straps, and one gilt metal bar on the shirt collar and side cap.
Lieutenants	One medium and one narrow, two medium or two medium with one narrow gold lace ring between, on the cuffs and shoulder straps and one or two silver bars or a gilt maple leaf on the shirt collar and side cap.
Captains and Commanders	Three or four medium gold lace rings on the cuffs and shoulder straps, and silver maple leaf or eagle on the shirt collar or side cap. Cap peak embroidered with one row of gold oak leaves.
Commodore (from May 1943)	One wide gold lace ring on the cuffs, and gold lace shoulder straps with one silver-embroidered five-pointed star. One five-pointed white metal star on the shirt collar and side cap.
Flag officers	One wide and one to three medium gold lace rings on the cuffs, and gold lace shoulder straps with two to four silver-embroidered five-pointed stars. Two to four five-pointed white metal stars on the shirt collar and side cap. On 14 December 1944 the rank of Admiral of the Fleet was introduced with four medium gold lace rings on the cuffs and five stars on the shoulder straps, shirt collar and side cap.

It was possible to distinguish the branch, special training, and branch or corps of naval personnel as follows:

Rank	*Line*	*Corps*
Ratings	White tape stripe on blue or blue stripe on white uniforms, round right sleeve seam.	Red tape stripe on blue and white uniforms, round left sleeve seam.
	Speciality badges worn on upper right sleeve.	Speciality badges worn on upper left sleeve.

Petty officers	Speciality and rate badges worn on right sleeve.	Speciality and rate badges worn on left sleeve.
Officers	Five-pointed star above rank distinction lace on cuffs and shoulder straps.	Corps badge above rank distinction lace on cuffs and shoulder straps, and in metal on left side of shirt collar (Warrant officer on both sides), and on left front of side cap.

Naval and Marine Aviation Cadets

Cadets wore naval warrant officers uniform with a special cap badge – a blue eagle and foul anchor superimposed on a yellow shield with blue border, and ensigned by the label 'Navy' in yellow. At first cadets wore a gold-embroidered five-pointed star on the ends of the jacket collar on both sides, but later this was changed to the foul anchor worn by cadets at Annapolis. United States Marine Corps Aviation Cadets wore a winged propeller on the ends of the collar on both sides, which were later worn on the shoulder straps.

United States Marine Corps

In 1912 a new 'green' service uniform was prescribed for marines in place of the existing khaki uniform, but due to production difficulties this uniform was not introduced until 1914. In 1929 it underwent further modifications.

The green service dress for officers is illustrated in 198. In 1942 the 'Sam Browne' belt for officers was replaced by a matching cloth belt with two-pronged metal buckle.

The peaked cap was made of matching green material with black leather peak and chin strap, and bronzed corps badge on the front. On the crown officers had a green lace quatrefoil. The campaign hat had a narrower brim than the army pattern, and the cords were green with a red fleck.

During the war the white undress uniform was replaced by a khaki drill service in the same cut, and badges and buttons as on the green uniform. All ranks also received the standard pattern light khaki drill side cap, shirt, and long trousers.

The blue dress uniform (195) continued to be worn during the war as a full dress or optional walking-out dress, by members of the marine detachments in Washington D.C. and London, England.

Combat uniform was basically the same as that of the U.S. Army [A.U. pp. 57–60 and 106, 152, 160 & 196] but had the Marine Corps emblem ensigned by the letters U.S.M.C. printed in black on the left breast pocket (197).

Marine Corps rank badges followed the army system, but varied in colour according to the colour of the uniform on which they were worn:

Uniform colour	Chevron colour
Blue	Yellow on red ground
Green	Green on red ground
Khaki	Green on khaki ground

Rank was indicated as follows:

N.C.O.s	Chevrons on both sleeves until September 1942 when they were ordered to be worn on the left sleeve only. Line n.c.o.s had arcs or 'rockers', while those on staff duties had straight 'ties'.
Warrant officers	As for naval warrant officers but with red enamel stripe.
Officers	As army.

Certain officers wore their branch badge on the collar as follows:

Paymaster dept	Crossed sword and quill surmounted by oak wreath.
Quartermasters dept	Crossed sword and key surmounted by blue enamel spoked wheel charged with thirteen stars.
Aide-de-camp to general officers	Shield of the United States set with one to three stars according to the rank of the general served.
Second Leader Marine Band	Silver lyre, which was also worn on the shoulder straps.

UNITED STATES OF AMERICA   Army Air Forces

On 20 June 1941 the air forces of the United States Army were officially placed under a centralised command and became the United States Army Air Forces (U.S.A.A.F.). It was not until 18 September 1947 that the air force became a separate arm with its own air force uniforms which were introduced in 1949.

As part of the army all personnel wore army uniforms with Air Corps emblem – a gilt metal winged silver propeller, and ultramarine and orange piping on the overseas cap.

On the upper left sleeve at shoulder height all ranks wore a circular blue shoulder sleeve insignia of the Army Air Forces, numbered Air Forces, or independent branch to which they belonged. These badges were predominantly light blue with designs in white, yellow, and red. Members of fighting formations began to wear their squadron insignia on the left front, or back of their flying jackets. U.S.A.A.F. ranks badges were those of the army. On 8 July 1942 the rank of Flight Officer was introduced, who wore an ultramarine and golden orange enamel bar.

The various branches of the U.S.A.A.F. were identified by silver aviation qualification badges or 'wings' which were worn on the left breast above the medal ribbons.

Before America entered the war she assisted the R.A.F. in a number of ways. American pilots volunteered for service with the R.A.F. and joined either British or the American Eagle Squadrons, whose badge was the American eagle ensigned by the letters 'E' and 's' in light blue on a grey ground, on the left sleeve at shoulder height. American technicians who had been recruited in the United States to do essential technical work in England, were issued with R.A.F. uniform with plain black plastic buttons, and 'U.S.A.' shoulder flash in light blue on dark blue ground. Americans also served with the Royal Canadian Air Force.

Aviation Cadets

In order to provide sufficient trained manpower for the air forces of the army, navy and Marine Corps, an Aviation Cadet Training programme was expanded and operated until finally curtailed in March 1944. Some aviation cadets wore army uniforms with a special winged-propeller cap badge, and light blue circular badge with a yellow winged-propeller on the right sleeve.

All appointments were indicated by either regular army or special cadet olive drab chevrons on dark blue-black ground on both upper sleeves. Cadet officers wore the army Reserve Officer Training Corps silver 'pips and diamonds' on the ends of the collar on both sides, but generally wartime shortages prevented the universal issue of special insignia to all cadets.

UNION OF SOVIET SOCIALIST REPUBLICS   Navy

Russian naval uniform developed along western lines, and the uniform worn during World War 2 originates from the middle of the last century.

Officers service dress is illustrated in 211. For work there was a single-breasted blue tunic or *kitel* with stand collar, five yellow metal buttons in front, patch breast and slash side pockets with three-pointed flap and button, and two small buttons at the back of the cuff on the outside. In hot weather officers wore a white cap cover, single-breasted white *kitel* with stand collar and five yellow metal buttons, open patch breast pockets and round cuffs. It was worn with white or blue long trousers, and white canvas or black leather shoes.

Warrant officers (*Mishman*) and chief petty officers (*Starshina*) wore officers uniform, while chief petty officers wore a special cap badge. The peaked cap with chief petty officers cap badge could also be worn with seamens dress by petty officers with more than five years' service.

Petty officers, midshipmen, and ratings wore the uniform illustrated in 213. For cold weather there was a long single-breasted blue greatcoat with six yellow metal buttons, or a short peacoat with two rows of six buttons.

At the beginning of the war rank badges were worn on the cuffs by all ranks. They were in gold on blue, or light blue on white uniforms for officers, and red or yellow on all uniforms for ratings. In January 1943 Tsarist-pattern shoulder straps were re-introduced for all ranks in all branches of the navy. Rank distinction lace on the cuffs was only retained by line officers on blue uniform only. On white uniform only shoulder straps were worn. As formerly line officers were known by naval, while those in other branches by army rank titles. Rank was indicated as follows:

Seamen	Five-pointed red star, or five-pointed red star edged with gold edging on both cuffs. From January 1943 plain pointed shoulder straps and shoulder patches, or shoulder straps and shoulder patches with one yellow lace bar.
Petty officers	Five-pointed red star with gold edging above one or two yellow lace bars on both cuffs. From January 1943 shoulder straps and patches with two or three yellow lace bars.

Note: Shoulder straps were worn on the peacoat and greatcoat, while shoulder patches in blue on blue, and white on white jumpers were worn by all ranks wearing square rig.

Chief petty officers	Five pointed red star with gold edging above two yellow lace rings on the cuffs. From January 1943 one wide yellow lace bar on the shoulder straps.
Midshipman	This title was derived from the English midshipman, but was known as a *Mishman*. He wore officers uniform with red star edged in gold above three yellow lace rings on the cuffs. From January 1943 wore blue shoulder boards with one wide gold lace stripe down the centre.
Lieutenants	Five-pointed gold star above one medium, one narrow above one medium, two medium, or one narrow above two medium gold lace stripes on the cuffs. From January 1943 gold lace shoulder straps on blue base with one blue stripe down the centre and one to four five-pointed silvered metal stars.
Captains	Five-pointed gold star above three or four medium or one wide gold lace stripe on the cuffs. From January 1943 gold lace shoulder straps on blue base with two blue stripes down the centre, and one to three five-pointed silvered stars. One row of gold oak leaves on the cap peak.
Flag officers	Large five-pointed red star edged in gold above one wide with one to four medium gold lace stripes on the cuffs. From January 1943 gold zigzag-pattern lace shoulder straps on blue base with one to four silver-

embroidered five-pointed stars on black ground. Gold embroidery on cap peak, and gold braid chin cords.

Prior to January 1943 rank distinction lace on the cuffs of the blue jacket, full-dress tunic, and greatcoat, either went all round the sleeve or was sewn on the outside only. On the blue working and white summer tunic, and on other types of working or semi-official uniforms, the stripes were only 6 cm (2·36 in.) long. After the re-introduction of shoulder straps, 6 cm (2·36 in.) long stripes were only worn on the blue jacket by line and line engineering officers.

The various corps were indicated as follows:

Corps	Lace	Colour	Badge	Cuff stripe
Line	Gold	Blue	–	Gold
Line engineering	Gold	Blue	Crossed wrench & hammer	Gold
Aviation	Gold	Light blue	–	Gold
Aviation engineering	Gold	Light blue	Crossed wrench & hammer	Gold
Coastal defence	Gold	Brown	–	–
Construction	Silver	Blue	Crossed wrench & hammer	–
Supply	Silver	Red	–	–
Medical with mil. training	Silver with green stripes	Red	Serpent & cup	–

The following corps wore narrow shoulder straps:

Medical without mil. training	Silver	Red	Serpent & cup	–
Veterinary	Silver	Red	Serpent & cup	–
Legal	Silver	Red	Shield on crossed swords	–
Administrative	Silver	Red	–	–

In addition naval aviators and flight engineers wore the same badges as their army counterparts on the upper left sleeve of their blue jackets.

There were no marines as such, but sailors serving on land were identified by a gold foul anchor on the upper left sleeve. Sailors serving alongside the army were often issued with army uniforms (217), with army rank badges and a yellow metal anchor on the shoulder straps.

UNION OF SOVIET SOCIALIST REPUBLICS
Military Air Force

The air force has been, since its formation at the beginning of this century, a branch of the army, and not an independent arm. In August 1924 a blue service uniform was introduced, and in December 1935, it underwent certain modifications, and was restricted for wear as a service, full, and walking-out dress. For everyday work and while flying army uniform was worn.

The blue service dress is illustrated in (220). The greatcoat was double-breasted with two rows of four brass buttons for officers, and single-breasted with five brass buttons for other ranks. The officer's version had slanting side pockets with flap, turn-back cuffs and half-belt at the back fastened with a button at each end.

In addition to the blue peaked cap and side cap or *pilotka* (221), there was a blue cloth helmet or *shlem*, which was later replaced by the fur cap or *ushanka*.

Air force personnel wearing army khaki uniforms were distinguished by light blue collar patches and piping, and later this colour also appeared on the shoulder straps.

Typical flying clothing is illustrated in 223 and 225. In anticipation of victory over Germany, new full-dress uniforms for air force generals and marshals were introduced in 1943 [A.U. 206].

Rank badges were those of the army [A.U. pp. 55–56], and were worn on light blue collar patches edged in gold for officers and black for political officers and other ranks. From January 1943 the following shoulder straps were introduced:

Other ranks	Light blue shoulder straps with black piping and gold or yellow lace stripes.
Officers	Gold lace shoulder straps on light blue base with light blue stripes and white-metal five-pointed stars according to rank.
Generals	Gold zigzag-pattern lace shoulder straps on light blue base with silver-embroidered five-pointed stars according to rank.

In 1924 embroidered badges for wear on the upper left sleeve were introduced as follows:

Aircraft pilots   Silver winged red star on gold twin-bladed propeller and crossed silver swords with gold hilts.

Airship pilots   Gold winged silver foul anchor with red star in the centre.

Mechanics   Silver winged red star on gold twin-bladed propeller and crossed gold hammer and spanner (introduced in 1925).

In August 1941 these badges were officially abolished.

YUGOSLAVIA   Royal and National Liberation Navies

The Yugoslav navy dates from the proclamation of the Kingdom of Yugoslavia in 1918, and naval uniform followed closely the pattern in general use. After the German invasion units of the Yugoslav navy served with the British Royal Navy, while towards the end of the war Tito's National Liberation Movement began to organise a naval force. Other elements of the Royal Yugoslav Navy continued to serve in the navy of the Independent State of Croatia.

The basic service dress for officers and petty officers is illustrated in 227. The greatcoat was double-breasted with two rows of five gilt metal buttons. In hot weather officers wore a white cap cover, open single-breasted white jacket with shoulder straps, long white trousers, and white canvas shoes.

In cold weather ratings wore a double-breasted peacoat. The hat was similar in shape to the German pattern, with blue or white top, black rayon ribbon with the name of the ship or installation, or in wartime *Ratna Monarica* in Cyrillic letters. Above the ribbon on the front was an oval metal cockade in the national colours – red, white, and blue.

Rank was indicated as follows:

Ratings   One to three white tape inverted chevrons on the upper left sleeve.

Petty officers   Blue cloth shoulder straps with one to three narrow gold lace stripes above four, four-pointed yellow metal stars arranged in a rhomboid.

Lieutenants	One, two, or two medium with one narrow between, or three medium gold lace rings with a curl on the only or uppermost on the cuffs. Gold lace shoulder straps with one blue stripe down the centre, and one to four four-pointed white metal stars.
Captains	One to three medium gold lace rings with a curl on the uppermost above one wide gold lace ring on the cuffs. Gold lace shoulder straps with two blue stripes down the centre, and one to three four-pointed white metal stars. One row of gold-embroidered oak leaves on the cap peak.
Flag officers	One medium gold lace ring with curl above one very wide gold lace ring on the cuffs. Above the curl one to three gold-embroidered six-pointed stars. Interwoven gold braid shoulder straps on blue base with one to three six-pointed silver metal stars. Two rows of gold-embroidery on the cap peak.

Ratings wore their trade badges in red above the rank chevrons on the upper left sleeve, while officers wore theirs in white metal on the shoulder straps.

The following branches were identified by coloured backing to the rank distinction lace as follows:

Corps	*Colour/Distinction*
Line	Uniform colour, and curl on the lace rings. Crowned foul anchor in white metal on the shoulder straps.
Commissioned warrant officers (*Equipage*)	Brown
Engineering	Silver grey
Construction	Purple
Administration	Scarlet
Medical	Uniform colour, and Aesculapius rod above curl.

Naval personnel serving with the British Royal Navy wore either Yugoslav naval uniform without shoulder straps on the jacket, or British uniform with 'Yugoslavia' on both sleeves at shoulder height. National Liberation Navy personnel wore the five-pointed red star on the headdress and the rank badges described in the air force section.

YUGOSLAVIA

The Royal Air Force was formed in 1930 as an independent service and received grey uniforms and special rank badges in 1938. After the German invasion Yugoslavs continued to serve in the newly-formed Croatian Air Force or with the R.A.F. in the Middle East, and later in Italy where towards the end of the war, the British helped build Tito's National Liberation Air Force, within the frame work of the Balkan Air Force.

The basic service dress for officers is illustrated in 230. The greatcoat was double-breasted with two rows of four gilt buttons, slanting side pockets with flap, and turn-back cuffs piped in black. In hot weather officers wore a white cap cover, and white version of the grey service dress.

Officers of the Anti-Aircraft Artillery Corps wore air force uniform but with black cloth tunic collar. Just above the black piped turn-back cuffs they wore gold-embroidered crossed cannon barrels ensigned by a winged bird. Rank badges were worn on grey cloth shoulder straps instead of on the cuffs.

Other ranks uniform was basically the same as officers, but was made of coarser cloth with white (sergeants yellow) metal buttons. Officers wore their rank badges on the cuffs and shoulder straps, while officers in the Anti-Aircraft Artillery Corps wore rank badges on the shoulder straps only.

Rank was indicated as follows:

Airmen	Pointed grey cloth shoulder straps with one or two four-pointed yellow metal stars.
Corporals	Pointed grey cloth shoulder straps with light blue piping and three four-pointed yellow metal stars.
Sergeants	Stiff light blue shoulder straps with one to three narrow gold lace stripes across the top, with below four four-pointed yellow metal stars arranged in a rhomboid.
Junior officers	One to three narrow gold lace stripes on the cuffs, and gold lace shoulder straps on a dark blue base with one dark blue stripe down the centre and one to four four-pointed silver stars.
Senior officers	One wide with one to three narrow gold lace stripes

	above on the cuffs, and gold lace shoulder straps on a dark blue base with two dark blue stripes down the centre and one to three four-pointed silver stars. One row of gold embroidery on the cap peak.
Generals	One to three large silver-embroidered stars on the tunic and greatcoat cuffs. Interwoven gold braid shoulder straps on light blue base with one to three six-pointed silver stars. Two rows of gold embroidery on the cap peak.

The following branches were distinguished as follows:

Branch	Distinction
Flying personnel	Gold-embroidered winged bird above the lace stripes for officers, and below the stars for generals, on the cuffs. Pilots badge in gilt metal which was worn above the right breast pocket.
Ground personnel	Plain lace stripes on the cuffs.
Engineering officers	Scarlet backing to the gold lace stripes, with gold-embroidered triangle within a circle above the lace stripes on the cuffs.
Anti-Aircraft Corps	Gold-embroidered crossed gun barrels ensigned by a winged bird on the cuffs. Tunic collar, piping, and *lampassen* in black.

Royalist personnel serving with the R.A.F. in the Middle East wore British uniform and rank badges, but with Yugoslav cap badge and flying badges.

Members of the Yugoslav National Liberation Air Force, which began to be formed in the Middle East and later in Italy, from 1943 onwards also wore British uniform and rank badges (229). Tito's men wore a number of different types of rank badges until the following system was finally standardised in May 1943.

N.C.O.s	One to three six-pointed white metal stars on the sleeves. Flight Sergeant three stars above a narrow stripe of silver lace.
Company officers	One to three six-pointed gilt metal or gold-embroidered stars above a stripe of narrow gold lace on the cuffs, and triangular collar patches.
Senior officers	One to three six-pointed gilt metal or gold-embroidered stars above two stripes of medium

| | gold lace on the cuffs, and collar patches in the shape of a rhomboid. |
| Generals | One to three six-pointed gilt metal or gold-embroidered stars above three stripes of wide gold lace on the cuffs, and collar patches in the shape of a rhomboid. |

This system also used by the National Liberation Navy.

NOTES TO PLATES

1. Belgium: Petty Officer (Second Maître), Belgium, 1940
Two patterns of cap tally are known to have existed; *Marinekorps* as illustrated, and *Marine* according to the regulations. Under the peacoat ratings wore a plain blue shirt and jumper.

2. Belgium: Air Force Captain (Capitaine), Belgium, 1940
The three stars on the collar denoted rank, and the lion on the left sleeve that the wearer had passed the A (highest) examination for pilots.

3. Belgium: Fighter pilot, Belgium, 1940
The one-piece flying overall was fastened diagonally in front with a zip-fastener and was usually worn without insignia of any kind.

4. Bulgaria: Air Force Captain Stefan Marinopolsky, 'Wildcat Squadron', 6th Fighter Regiment, Karlovo, August 1943
This shows the basic service dress for officers with German pattern collar patches and pilots wings on the right breast.

5. Bulgaria: His Majesty King Boris of Bulgaria, 1942
King Boris wears standard service dress for officers with full dress aiguillette. Rank was indicated both on the shoulder straps and on the cuffs

6. Bulgaria: Seaman, Black Sea, August 1941
This sailor wears the basic summer working rig. As in the Tsarist Russian

Navy the shirt was worn tucked into the trousers, and the trousers into the boots.

7. China: Air Force 2nd Lieutenant, 14th Squadron, Szechuan Province, 1939
The flying suit, helmet, and goggles were commercial types supplied by American manufacturers under contract. The map case is of Russian origin.

8. China: Admiral of the Fleet Chen Shao-Kwan, C.-in-C. Chinese Navy, London, 1943
During the war the black rank distinction lace was replaced by gold to make it more easily recognisable.

9. China: Air Force 2nd Lieutenant, 14th Squadron, Szechuan Province, 1939
Later in the war the field cap was replaced by a peaked cap with large embroidered cap badge. In 1940 rank badges were transferred from the cuffs to the shoulder straps.

Weapons: The dagger had a black grip, yellow metal fittings, and khaki sheath. The knot was made of black leather worked with silver wire for officers and gold for generals.

10. Denmark: Seaman (Matros), Denmark, 1940
The blue jumper was worn with white shirt with neck opening edged in blue, and black silk. The inscription on the hat tally was *KGL. Marine.*

11. Denmark: Commander (Orlog-skaptajn), Denmark, 1940
On the regulation greatcoat rank distinction lace was worn on the cuffs, and not on the shoulder straps as in most other navies.

12. Denmark: Air Force 2nd Lieutenant (Sekondløjtnant), Denmark, 1940
According to the regulations the uniform was that of the army, but most air force officers wore an open tunic with shirt and tie, instead of the pattern with high stiff collar.

13. Finland: Seaman (Matruusi) Cruiser Vainömöinnn, 1939
In addition to the rig illustrated there was a working dress which included a blue cloth side cap with black leather chin strap, and single-breasted tunic with stand-and-fall collar.

14. Finland: Fighter pilot, Finland, 1939
The flying suit was fur-lined, and was worn with either the felt boots illustrated, or fur-lined leather flying boots. **Weapons:** Finnish 9 mm. Lahti M.1940 automatic pistol.

15. Finland: Air Force Captain (Kapteeni) H. Kalima, June 1944
Regular officers and n.c.o.s could provide themselves with this blue uniform, but during the war most air force personnel wore army, or a combination of army and air force uniform. On the right breast he wears the Cross of Freedom 4th Class, and on the left the Graduate's Badge of the Regular Army Cadet School above the Pilots badge.

16. France: Quartermaster 2nd Class (Quartier-Maître 2ème Classe), Middle East, 1943
This tropical dress was introduced in 1925. This rating was a member of the Free French Navy and wears a British rating's money belt. Some ratings also wore the Cross of Lorraine in dark blue on the right breast.

17. France: Lieutenant (Lieutenant de Vaisseau) Jean Levasseur, March 1943
The Captain of the Free French ship *Alconit* wears standard service dress with rank distinction lace on the outside of the cuffs only (wartime economy measure) and the Free French badge on the right breast.

18. France: Chief Petty Officer (Maître), Cruiser La Gloire, 1940
In the left breast pocket of his working tunic he carries a notebook in which he wrote punishments for misdemeanours, and work to be carried out. Note the difference between the officers and petty officers cap badge.

19. France: Seaman (Matelot)
This gunnery rating wears the padded hood and heat-resistant gauntlets with typical working rig of striped shirt and linen working trousers.

20. France: Able Seaman (Matelot breveté), 1940
Ratings were known as *Cols bleus* and wore, in addition to the rig illustrated, a blue overall and matching side cap. On working clothing the rank badges were detachable.

21. **France:** Quartermaster 2nd Class (Quartier-Maître 2ème Classe), 1943

Under the peacoat is worn the jumper with blue jean collar, and under that the blue winter shirt. The anchor was only worn on the front of the best hat, and not on the everyday or working one.

Equipment: Standard French infantry pattern equipment.

Weapons: French 8 mm. M.1916 service rifle and M.1892 (modified) knife bayonet.

22. **France: Seaman 1st Company Fusilier Marine Commandos, London, 14 July 1942**

This unit later became part of the 10th (Interallied) Commando and participated in the Dieppe Raid. Just before embarking it was suggested that the 'France' flash should be removed in case the Germans treated captured French commandos as *francs-tireurs*, but all refused.

Equipment: Pattern 1937 web equipment and 'toggle rope', which could be joined with others to make a useful length of rope for scaling cliffs and so on.

Weapons: British .303 Bren light machine gun Mk. I.

23. **France: Lieutenant (Lieutenant de Vaisseau), 1st Battalion Fusilier Marine Commandos, England, 1944**

Uniform as illustrated in 22, but with the naval head-dress replaced by the green commando beret which was introduced in 1943, and the bronzed cap badge which followed in April 1944.

Equipment: Pattern 1937 web equipment; basic set for officers.

Weapons: British .455 Webley Mk. VI pistol No. 1.

24. **France:** Sub Lieutenant (Enseigne de Vaisseau 2ème Classe), Regiment March du Tchad, 2nd Free French Armoured Division (Division Leclerc), Normandy, June 1944

Here the basic combat dress of the U.S. Army is worn with French insignia and rank badges on the front of the jacket. Non-executive officers wore their rank badges on cloth tabs in their corps colour.

Equipment: Standard U.S. Army woven equipment.

25. **France: General (Commandant une Division) Valin, Bomber Command H.Q., High Wycombe, December 1944**

As Chief of the French Air Staff Valin wears a pre-war pattern leather flying jacket with his rank badges worn on a cloth tab on the front.

26. **France:** Colonel (Colonel), Berlin, August 1938

This officer wears the basic service dress, with full dress epaulettes, aiguillette, and dagger.

27. **France: Bomber pilot, France, 1940**

This shows the summer flying suit with distinctive stiffened brown leather helmet. The winter flying suit was made of fur-lined brown leather.

28. France: 2nd Lieutenant (Sous-Lieutenant), Alsace, 1944
U.S. Army khaki service dress came into use in the French Air Force from 1943 on. Rank was indicated on the cap and on the shoulder straps.

29. France: Major (Commandant) Louis Delfino, Normandy-Nieman Squadron of the Free French Air Force, East Prussia, January 1945
As squadron commander Delfino wears an Irving flying jacket supplied by Britain to Russia, with the coat of arms of Normandy painted on the left breast. On the blue jacket members of the squadron wore 'France' in white Latin letters on the left sleeve, and either 'France' or 'Normandy' in white Cyrillic letters on the right sleeve at shoulder height.

30. France: Private *(Soldat)*, Free French Air Force, Paris, 1944
The greatcoat is the standard pre-war pattern, while the beret which before the war was only worn with working dress, replaced the peaked cap.

Equipment: Standard French infantry pattern leather waist belt and ammunition pouches.

Weapons: French 8 mm. Fusil M.1907/15 service rifle.

31. Poland: Captain (Capitaine), Lyon-Bron, France, 1940
With the exception of the peaked cap which was specially made, the rest of the uniform was that of the French Air Force. The black leather coat was also supplied to and worn by Dutch aircrew.

32. Czechoslovakia: Sergeant-Major (Rotný), No. 310 (Czech) Squadron, R.A.F. Duxford, July 1940
French uniforms continued to be worn until British ones could be issued. Here Czech rank badges, as opposed to the French ones worn by the sergeant in 33, were worn. The Czech cap badge with swords was worn by combatants, and without swords by non-combatants.

33. Czechoslovakia: Sergeant (Sergent), Duxford, England, 1940
The other ranks version of the tunic or *vareuse* was worn with closed collar. On the right breast he wears both the Czech and French pilots badge. The latter was by tradition worn at a 45 deg. angle.

34. Germany: Leading Seaman (Obermaat), Channel Islands, 1941
The rank distinction lace on the collar patches was introduced on 1 December 1939, and the boarding cap in 1940. Civilian specialists *(Sonderführer)* wore a white metal foul anchor on the collar patches, and all buttons, badges, and lace were gold.

35. Germany: Admiral Carls, Gotenhaven (Gydnia), Autumn 1939
The white cap cover was officially worn between 20 April and 30 September, but was banned for wear in home waters during the war.

Weapons: M.1938 dagger in gilt metal with white ivory grip. It was worn suspended from two black *moiré* straps with gilt metal fittings. Officials had white metal hanger fittings.

36. Germany: Seaman (Matrose) Naval Assault Troop, Guernsey, July 1940

When serving on land seamen wore infantry pattern equipment and field-grey steel helmet with gold national emblem on a black shield on the left side.

37. Germany (Petty Officer (Bootsmann), Rome, 1943

The khaki brown tropical uniform was introduced in 1943, and was worn both on land and at sea. It included a side cap, tunic and short trousers made from the same material. For officers there were breeches and a peaked cap with matching cloth-covered peak.

38. Germany: Captain (Kapitän zur See), Langsdorff, Montevideo, December 1940

The captain of the pocket battleship (*Panzerschiff*) *Graf Spee* wore regulation whites with 1938 pattern open tunic, on which all buttons and badges were detachable.

Weapons: Naval officers sword (233).

39. Germany: Seaman (Matrose), Mediterranean, 1942

The white boarding cap, sports vest and working trousers with canvas shoes was a typical unofficial tropical rig.

Weapons: German .08 Parabellum automatic pistol.

40. Germany: Leading Seaman (Matrosengefreiter), Atlantic, 1942

This shows typical action rig with boarding cap instead of the more usual steel helmet. Life jackets came in a number of different patterns and colours, and included a yellow self-inflating type. It was quite common for the wearer's function to be painted in white letters (e.g. *Ob. Stm.* [*Obersteuermann*] or coxswain) on both sides of the jacket.

41. Germany: Sub-lieutenant (Oberleutnant zur See), England, 1945

During the war the white cap cover came to signify the captain. On his battle dress-type working blouse he wears the German Cross in Gold, and on the left the Iron Cross 1st Class. The trousers were part of the leather suit issued to U-boat crews.

42. Germany: Seaman (Matrose), U-67, Caribbean, February 1942

Grey or brown leather suits were issued to U-boat crews, and black ones to technicians who had to work in dirty conditions. Officers were distinguishable from ratings by having a three-quarter-length double-breasted leather jacket. During the war the wearing of flotilla or U-boat badges on the left side of the head-dress (40) became very popular. These badges were usually made from metal by the vessel's smiths.

43. Germany: Lieutenant (Kapitänleutnant), Coastal Artillery Battalion, Atlantic Wall, summer 1944

The field-grey peaked cap for officers and n.c.o.s had a black leather chin strap.

44. Germany: Seaman (Matrose), Naval Assault Troop, Westerplatte, September 1939

The regulation tunic illustrated differed from the army pattern by having a matching collar and slash side pockets instead of patch ones.

Equipment: Standard German army pattern waistbelt with brass or yellow metal buckle, and ammunition pouches.

Weapons: German Mauser Gew. 98k service rifle.

45. Germany: Admiral, north-western Germany, 1944

As commander of land-based naval troops (*Frontwerftmänner*) this admiral wears the naval version of the field-grey side cap, and army-pattern collar patches for general officers.

46. Germany: Staff-Sergeant (Oberwachtmeister), Naval Coastal Police, 1940

In 1940 the police cap badges and shoulder straps were replaced by the naval pattern, although the old type continued to be worn in Norway until the end of the war. On duty the gorget with luminous inscription *Marine-Küsten-Polizei*.

47. Germany: Chief Petty Officer (Oberbootsmann), Transport Fleet Speer, 1943

This organisation was an adjunct of the Legion Speer and assumed responsibility for the transportation of vital construction and engineering materials by river. Regulation uniform was introduced in 1943.

48. Germany: Kameradschaftsführer of the Naval Hitler Youth, Berlin, 1939

It is impossible to equate Hitler Youth ranks with those of other armed forces, but a youth would attain this rank at the age of fifteen and a half. The most important wartime function was to furnish replacements for the navy and merchant navy.

49. Germany: Lieutenant (Oberleutnant), Flying troops, Germany, 1940

This officer wears the 'flying blouse' and peaked cap which was identical for all officers in all branches up to the rank of General. Generals had gold piping and badges, and other ranks white metal badges and piping in *Waffenfarbe*.

50. Germany: Colonel General (Generaloberst) Erhard Milch, Berlin, August 1939

As State Secretary for Air and Inspector General of the Air Force Milch wears parade dress with cap. The sword or *Degen* was a special pattern awarded by Göring on promotion to general rank.

51. Germany: Major Wilhelm Elmer, Berlin, 1940

The greatcoat was worn open by all ranks. The lapels for general officers were in *Waffenfarbe*. Long unpiped trousers and shoes were worn with undress and walking-out uniforms.

Weapons: M.1937 dagger (238) for officers and officer candidates (*Oberfähnriche*). Generals had gilt metal fittings on the straps.

52. Germany: Major Helmut Wick, Commodore 2. 'Richthofen' Fighter Squadron, France, October 1940
Over his non-issue leather flying jacket he wears the self-inflating life jacket or *Schwimmweste*, and standard pattern flying boots made of black chrome leather and black suède.

53. Germany: Reich Marshal (Reichsmarschall) Hermann Göring, France, autumn 1940
As *Reichsmarschall* and C.-in-C. of the Air Force Göring wore a uniform of his own design. Under the rather civilian overcoat he wears a plain fly-fronted *Litewka* with large round fall collar. In his right hand he carries an *Interimstab*, which was in fact the everyday version of the marshal's baton.

54. Germany: Sergeant (Feldwebel) Aircrew, France, 1940
Illustrated here is the beige canvas one-piece summer flying suit with rank badges on the sleeves. Instead of the normal flying boots (52) he wears ordinary ankle boots.

55. Germany: Lieutenant (Ober-leutnant), Flying troops, Germany, 1944
Towards the end of the war there was a tendency to wear the collar of both the tunic and flying blouse closed at the neck, and to wear a small metal squadron badge either on the left lapel or on the left pocket as shown.

56. Germany: 2nd Lieutenant (Leutnant) Flying troops, East Prussia, 1944
The standardised M.1943 field cap was also issued to the air force. The flying jacket was one of many patterns worn by fighter pilots, and the so-called 'channel trousers' were fitted with large pockets to hold survival equipment in case of ditching at sea. They were usually worn with the trousers illustrated in 57.

57. Germany: Lieutenant (Ober-leutnant), Flying troops, Germany, 1944
The flying jacket had a detachable fur collar and was designed to be worn with the trousers illustrated in 56. On the belt he carries a compass.

58. Germany: Corporal (Unter-offizier), Flak Regiment 18, North Africa, March 1941
There was no special tropical greatcoat and all ranks wore the standard grey one. On the greatcoat n.c.o.s lace only appeared on the collar patches.

Weapons: German .08 or P.38 service automatic pistol.

59. Germany: Field Marshal (Generalfeldmarschall) Albert Kesselring, North Africa, August 1942
As C.-in-C. (*Oberbefehlshaber*) South, Kesselring wears standard Air Force tropical uniform, with rank badges appearing only on the shoulders. Above the left breast pocket he has the Operational Flying Clasp for reconnaissance squadrons, and on the pocket itself the 1939 Bar to the Iron Cross 1st Class, and Iron Cross 1st Class, and to the right the Pilot's Badge.

60. Germany: Lieutenant (Ober-leutnant), 27 Fighter Squadron, North Africa, June 1942
In addition to the issue German, captured British and Italian tropical uniforms, were also popular and often worn with German insignia.

Weapons: German Walther 7.65 mm. automatic pistol.

61. Russia: Captain (Kapitan) air unit of the National Committee for the Liberation of Russia (K.O.N.R.), Germany, 1945
Russian air crew serving with the *Luftwaffe* wore Air Force uniform with the badge of the Russian Army of Liberation (P.O.A.) or K.O.N.R. on the right sleeve, and oval metal cockade in the Russian national colours – blue, white, and red. Sometimes Russian pattern shoulder boards were also worn on *Luftwaffe* uniform.

62. Spain: Lieutenant Colonel (Teniente Coronel) Asaldo, 1941
Spanish Air Force personnel arriving in Germany were issued with *Luftwaffe* uniforms, on which they continued to wear Spanish decorations. On the upper right sleeve of both Spanish and German uniforms they then wore a woven shield in the Spanish national colours – red and yellow, on the upper right sleeve.

63. Belgium: N.S.K.K. man, National Socialist Motor Transport Corps Wallonie, Northern France, 7 July 1943
This unit was formed from members of the Rex (national movement named after the publishing house *Christus*

Rex) and A.G.R.A. (collaborationist group called *Les Amis du Grande Reich Allemand*) already serving in the German N.S.K.K. They wore *Luftwaffe* uniform with N.S.K.K. insignia and in this case the A.G.R.A. badge on the upper left sleeve.

64. Germany: Corporal (Oberjäger) 1. Parachute Rifle Regiment, Holland, May 1940
The parts of the uniform which were not covered by the smock, such as the steel helmet and trousers were field-grey, and not Luftwaffe grey. Parachute troops were classified as *Fliegertruppen* and so wore yellow *Waffenfarbe*.

Equipment: Standard infantry equipment with special fabric bag for the gas mask, and fabric bandoliers for additional ammunition and flare cartridges.

Weapons: German Schmeisser MP. 28, II sub machine gun and stick grenade 24.

65. Germany: General Bernard Ramcke, commander Rifle Brigade Ramcke, El Alamein, August 1942
The tropical peaked cap was issued with a neck flap *à la* French Foreign Legion, but was seldom worn. His decorations include the Knight's Cross, Bar to Iron Cross 1st Class, Iron Cross 1st Class, Wound Badge in black, and Baltic Cross.

66. Germany: Private (Jäger) 2. Parachute Rifle Regiment Crete, May 1941
The smock or 'bone sack' was issued in the same basic cut, but in olive

green, army pattern geometric (149) and blurred camouflage patterns, and sand-coloured material, depending on the theatre in which it was worn. It was worn over the equipment for the jump, and under it in action. Knee pads were worn outside the trousers, and bindings inside, because the landing position (all fours) adopted initially caused many landing injuries.

67. Germany: Grenadier, Grenadier Regiment, Hermann Göring Division, Sicily, 1943

Members of this division were issued with Waffen-SS camouflage smocks and helmet covers. The rest of the tropical uniform was standard *Luftwaffe*.

68. Germany: Lieutenant General (Generalleutnant) Schimpff, Normandy, July 1944

As commander of the 3.Parachute Division he wears the M.43 field cap with unofficial divisional badge on the left side. The jacket is the special *Luftwaffe* pattern for field formations, and the trousers and boots are the parachute pattern.

69. Germany: Sergeant Major (Hauptfeldwebel) Panzer Regiment 'Hermann Göring', Berlin-Reinickendorf West, summer 1943

Members of the tank regiment and assault gun battalion wore the black tank uniform illustrated, with the pink piping appearing only on the shoulder straps. All other piping on cap and collar patches was in white. The two lace rings on the cuffs denote that the n.c.o. is acting as Company Sergeant Major (*Stabsfeldwebel*).

70. Estonia: German Anti-Aircraft Helper, Copenhagen, 1945

This special uniform originally introduced for members of the Hitler Youth assisting the *Luftwaffe*, was later issued to foreign youths who wore a diamond-shaped cap badge and armlet in their national colours. Rank was indicated on the shoulder straps.

71. Germany: Leader (Luftschutzführer) Air Protection Service, Germany, 1939

The original uniform of the German equivalent to the British A.R.P. was replaced during the war by the uniform illustrated in 69. Rank (five non and four commissioned) was indicated on the collar patches and shoulder cord.

Weapons: M.1935 leaders dagger.

72. Germany: 2nd Lieutenant (Leutnant) Air Protection Police, Germany, 1944

In 1942, the full-time and highly mobile Security and Help Service was transferred to the Order Police and became the *Luftschutzpolizei*. Its personnel continued to wear air force uniform but with police insignia and rank badges.

73. Australia: Able Seaman R. Peet, *H.M.A.S. Australia*, London

This gunnery rating 3rd class wears standard Royal Navy 'square rig'. The trousers were kept rolled in a kit bag when not in use, and were sometimes pressed in this fashion, although it was not obligatory.

74. Great Britain: Admiral of the Fleet Sir Dudley Pound, G.C.B., G.C.V.O., August 1941

As First Sea Lord and Chief of Naval Staff he wears standard officers uniform with the so-called 'monkey jacket' or reefer.

75. Great Britain: Petty Officer, side party, England, 1940

This Bosun's mate wears 'fore an aft rig' with petty officers cap badge. On his left sleeve he wears his rate badge above three red inverted chevrons which denoted thirteen or more years of service, or in naval parlance 'undetected crime'.

76. New Zealand: Sub Lieutenant R. Hooker R.N.Z.V.R. *H.M.S. Emperor*, summer 1944

Some officers wore their rank distinction lace on khaki drill slides on the shoulder straps provided with the shirt or bush jacket, while others wore blue shoulder straps as illustrated. It was not uncommon to see a narrow blue cloth slide with 'Royal Navy' in white around the base of the khaki shoulder straps.

77. Great Britain: Lieutenant Commander, Malta, 12 September 1943

This officer wears the standard M.1901 white uniform with black leather gaiters which were worn with certain orders of dress on land.

Weapons: M.1891 naval officers sword.

78. Great Britain: Leading Seaman (Air) A. L. Johnson D.S.M., H.M.S. *Ark Royal*, October 1941

'Ginger' wears the M.1938 tropical dress for members of the seaman branch. Other miscellaneous junior ratings wore ordinary collar attached shirt. A sun helmet with hat ribbon or badge was also worn with this rig. On-board ship a blue canvas, and on land a white canvas one were authorised.

79. Great Britain: Leading Seaman, Atlantic Ocean, 1942

This leading gunnery rating wears the anti-flash hood under the blast-proof and steel helmets, and special gauntlets. The inflatable life belt was equipped with a red light operated from a four and a half volt drycell battery.

80. Great Britain: Coxwain, Petty Officer (unconfirmed), *H.M.S. Trusty (Submarine L.52)*

The blue overall was just one of many kinds of working clothes. The 'stoke hole' boots were often worn without laces so they could be kicked off before jumping into the sea. In addition to the standard H.M.S. hat tallies, others with 'H.M. Submarine' or 'H.M. Minesweeper' could be purchased from the Purser's clothing store or 'slops' or from naval outfitters.

81. Great Britain: Signalman (communications branch), North Sea, 1943

This 'bunting tosser' wears an issue duffle coat, which were also produced in dark blue and white. The binoculars which formed part of the watch keeping equipment are marked with the white arrows which indicated government property. The signal flags were dark blue when the sun was behind the sender, or white when in front.

82. Great Britain: Lieutenant F. R. C. Smith RN, England, 1943
Smith wears the waxed Egyptian cotton 'Barber' suit, which like the 'Sladden' suit were named after the designer. On his beret he wears the peaked cap badge.

Equipment: Pattern 1937 web equipment set for Royal Armoured Corps personnel.

Weapons: British Sten Mk II sub machine gun with modified foregrip, and U.S. Calibre .45 M.1911 A 1 automatic pistol.

83. Great Britain: Captain, Anzio, January 1944
The blue battle-dress was introduced in late 1943, and on the left sleeve he wears the Combined Operations flash. The letters on the side of the steel helmet indicate that this officer was Senior Naval Officer Liaison.

84. Great Britain: Seaman, Portsmouth, 1943
This sentry wears the standard hat tally and issue greatcoat which had either black plastic or brass buttons painted black, and was worn without insignia.

Equipment: Pattern 1908 web equipment.

Weapons: British Rifle No. 1 S.M.L.E. Mk III* and Mk I bayonet 1907.

85. Great Britain: Able Seaman, Naval Beach Party, Alexandria, 1943
During the war khaki drill was worn more often than white clothing by both officers and ratings. Members of Naval Beach Parties often wore the letters 'NBP' on the front of the steel helmet, or on an armlet.

Equipment: Pattern 1908 equipment, with the 1913 modification to the lower ammunition pouches on the left side only, which prevented them from opening unintentionally when crawling.

Weapons: British Rifle No. 1 S.M.L.E. Mk. III* and Mk I bayonet pattern 1907.

86. Great Britain: Commander A. E. W. Willmot R.N.V.R., Courseulles, Normandy, June 1944
As Resident Naval Officer in Charge of the port, Willmot wears army battle dress with R.N.R. shoulder straps, and naval peaked cap.

Equipment: Pattern 1937 web equipment basic set for officers.

Weapons: British Webley .455 Mark VI Pistol No. 1.

87. Great Britain: Leading Seaman, Naval Beach Party, England, 1943
On army battle-dress this 'hooky' wears 'Royal Navy' shoulder flashes, Combined Operations flash, leading seaman's rate badge, and invented chevron for at least five years' service.

The signallers attached to beach parties also wore the shoulder flash 'Beach Signals'.

88. Great Britain: Air Gunner, Fleet Air Arm, England, November 1940

The flying suit is the M.1940, with detachable fur collar, and the Type D tan cape sheepskin gauntlets lined with stockinette fleece. The Type C wired naval helmet is here worn with Mk. 4 goggles.

Weapons: British Vickers .303 G.O. (gas operated) machine gun.

89. Great Britain: Lieutenant Commander D. Brooks R.N.V.R., Fleet Air Arm Branch.

The letter 'A' inside the curl denoted F.A.A. and was introduced in 1939, and the flying badge for trained pilots in 1925. The badge for observers followed in 1942. The Type C wired naval helmet is worn with Mk. 5 goggles and standard life saving waistcoat.

90. Great Britain: Upper Yardsman, Fleet Air Arm Branch, *H.M.S Sparrow-Hawk* (land training establishment), March 1942

The white hat band denoted officer cadet, and replaced the standard patterns with either 'F.A.A.' or 'Fleet Air Arm'. Here are worn the Irving flying jacket and 1941 pattern boots with socks rolled over the top.

91. Great Britain: Bugler Royal Marines, 1943

The bugler, who was trained to play drum and fife as well, is here wearing

embarkation order with the Wolseley helmet.

Equipment: 1937 pattern web equipment.

92. Great Britain: Captain Desmond Dillon, Royal Marines, Southsea, 1945

Blue battle-dress (here worn with service dress trousers) was first issued to crews of landing craft, but was later also worn as an everyday or working dress. The other ranks pattern was always worn closed at the neck.

93. Great Britain: Royal Marine, Madagascar, May 1942

At first the fabric belt was in the Royal Marines colours, but during the war it was replaced by the standard naval pattern in blue. In February 1942 long puttees were officially to have been replaced by short ones.

Equipment: Pattern 1908 web equipment.

Weapons: British Rifle No. 1 S.M.L.E. Mk. III* and Mk. I bayonet pattern 1907.

94. South Africa: Seaman, Alexandria, June 1942

This rating wears the M.1938 tropical dress with South African hat tally.

95. Ceylon: Boy R.N.V.R., Ceylon, 8 May 1942

Ratings undergoing basic training wore the blue drill shirt and shorts as illustrated. The hat tally reads 'R.N.V.R. CEYLON'.

Equipment: Pattern 1908 web belt and bayonet frog.

Weapons: British Rifle No. 1 S.M.L.E. Mk. III* and Mk. I bayonet pattern 1907.

96. India: Able Seaman (Senior Telegraphist) Karunakaran Maniath, *H.M.S. Carnatic*

The puggree was permitted as an alternative head-dress on racial or religious grounds, and is here worn by a Sikh. The hat tally 'H.M.I.S.' is wound into the *puggree*, while those entitled to a cap badge wore it pinned on the front of the *puggree*.

97. Great Britain: Flight Sergeant, England, 1940

This shows the basic service dress of the R.A.F. with the wings or Albatross worn on both sleeves at shoulder height by all other ranks. This badge was also worn by dominion and colonial air forces although the design varied considerably.

98. Great Britain: Air Marshal Sir Hugh Dowding, 28 June 1940

As Air Officer Commanding Fighter Command Dowding wears service dress with the special pattern side cap for air officers.

99. Great Britain: Acting Wing Commander Henry Cribb, D.F.C., No. 35 Squadron R.A.F.

Although tried out as early as 1939, the air force version of the battle-dress was not generally issued until 1943. It differed from the army pattern only in that the breast pocket flaps were three-pointed and not pointed. The ribbon of the D.F.C. was worn under the wings on the left breast.

100. Great Britain: Squadron Leader, Rangoon, 26 August 1945

As Deputy Provost Marshal this officer wears jungle green uniform with grey side cap, and armlet prescribed.

Equipment: Pattern 1937 web belt and pistol holster (probably of Indian manufacture).

Weapons: British .38 No. 2 Mk. 1* pistol.

101. Great Britain: Wing Commander Barry Heath, Middle East, 1943

The khaki drill bush jacket with long or short sleeves, and shorts or long trousers was the most popular form of tropical clothing. The pre-war Wolseley helmet with flash in the R.A.F. colours on the left side was seldom worn during the war.

102. Great Britain: Aircraftsman, Jerusalem, 22 April 1943

According to regulations insignia, such as the propeller for leading aircraftsmen, and various shoulder flashes like the one for the R.A.F. Regiment were in red on khaki drill ground, for wear on light khaki clothing.

103. Great Britain: Aircraftsman, England, 1942

Fitters usually wore rubber-soled boots so as not to damage the aircraft on which they climbed, and so were nicknamed 'pansies'. The side cap was also often used as a tool bag.

104. Great Britain: Flight Lieutenant, England, 1944
This fighter pilot has stuffed his maps into 1943 pattern flying boots, which were ordinary laced black leather sheepskin lined walking shoes, stitched to which were a black suède leg portion. In event of forced landing in enemy territory, the upper part could be detached from the shoe by means of a small knife provided.

105. Great Britain: Sergeant, England, 1944
Over his battle-dress he wears the standard self-inflating life saving waistcoat. The Type C general purpose flying helmet was made of brown chrome leather with chamois lining, and the goggles were fitted with anti-flare lenses.

106. New Zealand: Flying Officer A. Carr, England, 1945
The flying helmet is the type C wired, and over his battle-dress he wears the standard life jacket (Type LS yellow). Gauntlets (not shown) were made of tan cape sheepskin with stockinette fleece lining, and could be worn over silk or chamois leather gloves, or knitted gloves or mittens.

107. Australia: Aircrew (Lancaster bombers), spring, 1944
The standard 1941 pattern buoyant suit was made of yellow aerocord and could be worn over a kapok lining with electrically heated gloves and boots. According to regulations the correct foundation for flying clothing was a white roll-necked knitted pullover worn over the trousers, and under the jacket, with the trousers

tucked into white knitted socks. The flying boots are the 1941 pattern with brown rubber soles and brown suède uppers. Between the outer suède and sheepskin lining was a splinter-proof interlining of thirty layers of parachute silk.

108. Great Britain: Beaufighter pilot, England, 1941
This type of two-point detachable parachute with integral harness was introduced before the war, but at the beginning was restricted to all flying personnel including at first the whole crews of flying boats, other than pilots of single-engined land planes. It was later used primarily for training purposes. The helmet is the type C general purpose.

109. Iraq: Sergeant Iraq Levies, Egypt, 1944
Originally formed as a frontier force, it was then used as an air defence formation under British officers who wore R.A.F. tropical uniform with slouch hat and crossed *Kungars* (ornamental dagger) cap badge. Note the red albatross and army pattern rank chevrons.

110. Great Britain: Leading Aircraftsman Bob Cook, No. 2 Armoured Car Company, Palestine, 1939
Apart from the uniform illustrated armoured car crews also wore a blue overall with short sleeves and legs. Rank chevrons were either the army pattern, or made of white tape.

Equipment: 1908 pattern web belt and holster.

Weapons: British Webley .455 Mark VI Pistol No. 1.

111. Great Britain: Leading Aircraftsman, Royal Air Force Regiment, England, May 1943
Since its formation in February 1942 members of the R.A.F. Regiment wore army clothing with R.A.F. rank badges.

Equipment: 1937 pattern web equipment, blancoed according to the whim of the commander or availability of blanco. According to regulations it was to have been grey.

Weapons: British .303 S.M.L.E. rifle and No. 4 bayonet.

112. Great Britain: Observer, Royal Observer Corps, England, February 1944
Grey battle-dress and black beret were introduced in June 1941, and replaced the civilian clothing and armlet worn hitherto. The pram was used to push around the telephone unit which provided the main contact between post and command.

113. Great Britain: Aircraftsman, Balloon Barrage Section, Thames Estuary, January 1940
The dress illustrated was worn over R.A.F. uniform when on duty on water.

114. Great Britain: Cadet, No. 14 (Uxbridge) A.T.C. Squadron, May 1943
This cadet wears the obsolete pattern of R.A.F. service dress with stand-and-fall collar. All badges and buttons etc. were in chromed metal, and the squadron badge (embroidered in light blue on grey) was worn on both sleeves at shoulder height.

115. Australia: Flight Lieutenant D. J. Shannon D.F.C., No. 617 (Dambusters) Squadron R.A.F., June 1943
Shannon wears R.A.F. rank distinction lace instead of the regulation Australian gold pattern. Australians also wore the blue version of the battle-dress.

116. New Zealand: Flight Lieutenant Les Munro, No. 617 (Dambusters) Squadron R.A.F., June 1943
Over his service dress, which was usually the second best one, he wears the Type LS yellow life saving waistcoat or life jacket. On his upper left sleeve he wears the 'New Zealand' flash.

117. South Africa: Major Malcolm Osler D.F.C., No. 1 Squadron S.A.A.F., North Africa 1941
Those South Africans who volunteered for service outside the Dominion wore the orange flash on their shoulder straps. All badges and buttons were in bronzed metal.

118. Canada: Flight Lieutenant, Royal Canadian Air Force, Ottawa, December 1941
This beaver-skin cap was worn in winter by officers, while other ranks had a cloth winter cap with ear flaps. The extreme winter in Canada necessitated the development of special winter flying clothing which included fur overalls.

119. United States of America: Flying Officer Andrew Mamedorf, No. 609 (West Riding) Squadron R.A.F., autumn 1940

On 19 September 1940 No. 71 (Eagle) Squadron of the R.A.F. was formed in Church Fenton from American volunteers, who like Mamedorf had been serving in other squadrons. As members of the Volunteer Reserve they wore 'V.R.' on the tunic collar and greatcoat shoulder straps, and from 13 October 1940 the Eagle Squadron badge on the upper left sleeve.

120. Sierra Leone, British West Africa: Leading Aircraftsman A. K. Hyde, January 1943

Aircrew cadets wore the white distinction as illustrated on the side cap, and a white disc behind the cap badge on the peaked cap. Officer cadets wore a white band round the headdress.

121. Norway: Captain Dagkron, England, April 1942

Although similar to the uniform of the R.A.F. the Norwegian Air Force in England introduced its own uniforms in 1941, which differed as follows: Norwegian cap badge, dark blue piped pointed cuffs, bronzed buttons, and Norwegian rank badges on the collar.

122. Poland: Flight Lieutenant Florian Martini, No. 317 (Wilno) Squadron P.A.F., Northolt, March 1944

All Polish officers were enrolled in the R.A.F. Volunteer Reserve with the rank of Flight Lieutenant, but continued to wear their former Polish rank on the collar.

123. France: Flight Sergeant (Sergent-Chef), Liverpool, 1943

This regular French Air Force n.c.o. serving as an instructor at the parachute school at Ringway, wears British battle-dress with French rank badges on the shoulder straps and front of the blouse.

124. Greece: Vice Admiral (Antinávarkhos) P. Voulgaris, Jerusalem, 22 April 1944

As C.-in-C. Greek Navy, Voulgaris wears basic service dress which resembles closely that of the British Royal Navy.

125. Greece: Petty Officer 2nd Class (Ipokeleftiś B), Greece, 1941

Service dress is basically the same as for officers, with the exception of the cap badge and rating badges on the sleeve. The propeller under the chevron denoted mechanic.

126. Greece: Air Force Corporal (Lohias), Greece, spring, 1941

This shows the basic issue service dress for other ranks. Officers and senior n.c.o.s wore an open tunic and peaked cap based on the British model.

127. Hungary: Vitéz (Hero) Captain (Százados) Julius Horváth, Hungary, 1944

The winged bird also appeared on the left side of the side cap. As an alternative to the laced field boots, officers wore black boots with gold lace around the top and circular yellow metal cockade on the front.

Weapons: Hungarian Frommer 7.65 mm. automatic pistol.

128. Hungary: Lieutenant General (Vezefökapitany) Horthy, Hungary, 1939

There were no admirals as such in the Hungarian river forces, but as Regent of Hungary, and former Austrian naval officer, Horthy assumed the rank and title of Vice Admiral. The red star on the right breast is the Turkish War Medal or Iron Half Moon instituted in 1915.

129. Hungary: Air Force Corporal (Örvezetö) near Kiev, Russia, August 1941

In addition to the hat illustrated, air force personnel also had a side cap. The winged propeller badge was worn on the tunic and greatcoat collar by all other ranks.

Weapons: Hungarian Frommer .380 M.1939 automatic pistol.

130. Italy: Seaman (Marinaio), Bordeaux, May 1941

This rating wears the basic working dress with beret.

131. Italy: Vice Admiral (Ammiraglio Designato di Armata) Count Riccardi, Italy, 1940

As Under Secretary for State for the Navy Riccardi wears officers service dress with full dress sash. Aide-de-camps wore the sash over the left shoulder. The sceptre and crown under the rank badges on the cuffs

signified that the wearer held a command.

Weapons: M.1861 naval officers sword.

132. Italy: Lieutenant Commander (Capitano di Fregatta) Gino Spagone, commander of the submarine 'Guglielmotti', Bordeaux, May 1941

Spagone wears regulation cap with rank distinction lace, leather jacket issued to submariners, and leather sea boots. The absence of rank badges anywhere but on the cap was not typical.

133. Italy: Seaman (Marinaio) Naples, 1944

This rating wears the summer jumper with blue trousers instead of the white ones. The silk and lanyard were tied in many different ways. The standard hat tally had *Regia Marina* in gold lettering on it.

134. Italy: Admiral Pavesi, Sicily, June 1943

As C.-in-C. Italian naval forces on the island, Pavesi wears a *sahariana* with naval cap and trousers. The *sahariana* was a popular garment in all three services, and was also often worn by German and allied personnel.

135. Italy: Captain (Commandante) Alberto Campanella, August, 1941

As captain of the *Zoea* Campanella wears a typical white overall and cap with white cover. This officer was also awarded four silver and three bronze medals for bravery, as well as the German Iron Cross 2nd Class.

136. Italy: Marine, Ligurian Coast, 1943
The standard naval summer jumper illustrated in 133, is here worn with white shorts. The gaiters are similar to the British pattern.

Equipment: Web equipment similar to the British 1908 pattern was supplied by Britain under contract, and was then produced in Italy under licence.

Weapons: Italian 7.35 mm. Model 38 TS carbine.

137. Italy: Lieutenant Commander (Capitano di Corvetta) Umberto Bardelli, commander of the Barbarigo Battalion of the Decima Flottiglia MAS, Nettuno front, April 1944
Bardelli wears the M.1943 field uniform originally introduced for parachute troops. Rank badges appear on the beret and cuffs, and the shield-shaped badge of the *Decima* on the left sleeve. Above the medal ribbons is the circular gilt badge for submariners.

138. Italy: Boy with mascot, Decima Flottiglia MAS, October 1944
The boy wears the grey-green version of the blue jumper with matching trousers, which were originally issued to marines before the introduction of the uniform illustrated in 137 above.

Equipment: Special canvas pouches for forty-round sub machine gun magazines.

Weapons: Italian 9 mm. Beretta M.1938A sub machine gun.

139. Italy: Captain (Capitano) Vittorio Mussolini, Yugoslavia, 5 May 1941
The son of the Italian dictator, who was soon to die on a proving flight, wears the standard flying suit with rank badges on the cuffs, although they were also often worn on the left breast above a squadron badge.

140. Italy: General (Generale d'Armato) Valle, Berlin, August 1939
As State Secretary for Air, Valle wears service dress with the military pilots wings above the medal ribbons on the left breast. Two badges above the rank badges on the cuffs indicated promotion for meritorious conduct in action.

141. Italy: 2nd Lieutenant (Sottotenente), May 1942
The same flying suit as illustrated in 139 above, is here worn with rank badges on the cuffs and on the sides of the flying helmet.

142. Italy: Captain (Capitano), Middle East 1940
The standard flying suit for wear in hot climates was made of white linen, as was the helmet. The life jacket was filled with kapok.

143. Italy: Marshal (Maresciallo dell 'Aria) Italo Balbo, Tobruk, 1940
As C.-in-C. Italian forces in North Africa, Balbo wears typical tropical dress, although the wearing of riding boots with shorts was unusual. On the *sahariana* the shoulder straps were detachable.

144. Italy: 2nd Lieutenant (Sotto-tenente), North Africa, 1940
This officer wears the pre-war white tropical uniform with full-dress sash and aiguillette for A.D.C.s.

Weapons: M.1924 officers sword.

145. Italy: Corporal (Primo aviere) Air Transport Group Terracciano, Helsinki, April 1944
This was the basic service dress for other ranks of both the Royal and Republican air forces. The unofficial wings were normally worn on the right breast.

146. Italy: Lieutenant Colonel (Tenente Colonello) Baylon, Bellagio (Como), September 1944
As Chief of Staff of the Republican Air Force, Baylon wears officers service dress with field cap with new pattern badge, and *gladio* on the tunic collar.

147. Italy: Lieutenant (Tenente) Gazzotti, Padre of the Torpedo Bomber (Aerosiluranti) Group, Lonate (Varese), April 1944
On his cassock collar 'Padre Siluro' wears the republican *gladio* and rank badges on purple backing.

148. Italy: Private (Aviere) Arditi Parachute Regiment, Tradate (Varese), February 1944
The smock was made of Italian-camouflage material, and the helmet was a special parachutist model. Boots were identical to the German front-lacing pattern.

Weapons: Italian 9 mm. Beretta M.1938A sub machine gun, and second pattern *M.S.V.N.* dagger.

149. Italy: Lieutenant (Tenente) Franco Tomasina, Folgore Parachute Regiment, Italy, 1944
Tomasina wears a German parachutists smock in the geometric camouflage pattern, with *gladio* on the collar and rank badges on the left breast.

Equipment: Binoculars, straps supporting and waistbelt are German, with special belt buckle introduced for republican parachute troops.

150. Italy: Sergeant (Sergente) Folgore Parachute Regiment, Italy, 1944
The M.1943 field uniform is here worn with regimental collar patches, and cuff-band '*Per l'onore d'Italia*' (For the honour of Italy) which was adopted by parachutists who remained loyal to Mussolini after the armistice.

151. Japan: Petty Officer 2nd Class (Nitō Heisō), Japan, 1940
This shows the basic service dress for petty officers with white cap cover.

Weapons: Japanese 6.5 mm. Type 38 rifle.

152. Japan: Commander (Chūsa) Atsugi airport, Japan, 1945
This tunic replaced the old pattern with stand collar and black lace trimming, and was worn without collar patches, but with shoulder straps, and from January 1944 the new pattern rank badges on the cuffs.

Weapons: Japanese officers *Seki* style sword.

153. Japan: Probationary Seaman, Japan, 1940
The basic 'square rig' was as illustrated, although the socks and sandals

were just one of many different kinds of footwear. With full dress or landing rig, ratings wore white canvas gaiters.

154. Japan: Vice Admiral (Chūjō) Ie Shima, near Okinawa, 19 August 1945

As naval aide to vice chief of the Japanese General Staff Kawabe, this flag officer wears typical wartime naval olive drab uniform with two blue stripes on his cap (all commissioned officers), and rank badges on his lapels.

Weapons: Japanese officers *Tachi*-style sword.

155. Japan: Admiral (Taishō) Yamamoto, C.-in-C. Imperial Japanese Navy, Tokyo, 1941

He wears regulation 'whites' with white cap cover, and on his left breast the Grand Cross breast star of the Order of the Rising Sun.

Weapons: Naval officers undress dirk.

156. Japan: Petty Officer 2nd Class (Nitō Heisō), Japan, 1940

The white working uniform was worn by both petty officers and ratings and was made of linen. There were also other kinds of working clothing including one-piece overalls.

157. Japan: Petty Officer 2nd Class (Nitō Heisō), Saigon, 1945

He wears typical wartime naval olive drill uniform, which was also worn by marine personnel. His rate badge is visible on the right sleeve, although there were instances of these badges also being worn on the left.

Equipment: Standard Japanese army pattern field equipment [A.U. 235].

Weapons: Japanese 7.7 mm. Type 99 long rifle [A.U. 253].

158. Japan: Lieutenant (Tai-i), Wake Island, 4 September 1945

On the cap all officers wore two rings (blue on khaki or white caps and yellow on blue caps), while ratings wore only one ring. During the war caps were issued which did not have these rings. Collar patches were detachable.

Weapons: Japanese officers *Tachi*-style sword.

159. Japan: Petty Officer 1st Class (Ittō Heisō), Naval Aviation Service, Japan, 1946

This naval pilot, who test-flew Japanese aircraft for Allied Technical Air Intelligence, wears a sailors shirt under the standard summer two-piece flying suit, with rating badge on the left breast.

160. Japan: Cadet Air Force Academy, Japan, 1940

For basic training cadets wore army uniform and equipment, but were distinguished by the insignia on the collar.

Equipment: Standard Japanese infantry equipment.

Weapons: Japanese 7.7 mm. Type 99 long rifle [A.U. 253].

161. Japan: 2nd Lieutenant (Shoi) Iso Tani, Pacific Ocean, 1944-45

On the sleeves of the standard flying suit pilots wore the Japanese flag with

Kami Kaze written in Japanese characters. The pilot's name was written on the parachute harness.

Weapons: Japanese officers *Tachi*-style sword, which was carried in the cockpit.

162. Japan: Ground crew, Japan, 1940

Normally a cap with ear flaps was worn with the working overall. Notice the mechanic's badge on the left breast pocket.

163. The Netherlands: Torpedo Artificer 1st Class William Breertjes, England, 27 March 1942

The yellow chevron was the rate badge of a *Korporaal*, and on the left sleeve he would have worn crossed torpedoes in yellow. The hat tally is the old pattern in Gothic script.

164. The Netherlands: Lieutenant (Luitenant ter Zee 1e Klasse), Naval Air Service, England, 1942

The uniform is the basic naval officers service dress, with winged radial engine on the cap badge and collar, which identifies his branch. The badge on the left breast denotes pilot observer.

165. The Netherlands: 2nd Lieutenant (2e Luitenant), Holland, May 1940

This officer wears army service dress with light blue piping and radial engine and propeller badge on the collar.

Weapons: Belgian Browning Long 9 mm. automatic pistol.

166. The Netherlands: Marine, Far East, 1945

This marine wears U.S. Marine clothing and equipment with Dutch Marine Corps badge on the left breast.

Equipment: Standard American woven equipment.

Weapons: U.S. .30 M1 carbine.

167. The Netherlands: Sergeant Major (Sergeant-Majoor), Royal Marine Corps, England, 23 March 1944

Here is worn the full dress uniform, with rank chevrons on the cuffs.

Weapons: Standard naval pattern cutlass.

168. The Netherlands: Sergeant Major (Sergeant-Majoor), Royal Marine Corps, Aruba (lesser Antilles), 1940

The grey-green tropical uniform could be worn with the slouch hat illustrated, peaked or field cap, or M.1928 steel helmet. He wears British Fox puttees. The collar patches with rank distinction lace were also worn on the white uniform.

Equipment: Standard infantry pattern equipment with gas mask on the left and pouch to hold circular magazines for the British .30–06 Lewis light machine gun.

169. Norway: Private (Menig flyver), Norway, 1940

The uniform is that of the Norwegian army, with only the green piping to indicate that he belongs to the air service.

170. Norway: Lieutenant (Löjtnant), Norway, 1940

Rank was indicated by the cap badges on the side cap which was worn by air service personnel only, and by the stars on the collar. On the right breast he wears the military pilots wings.

Equipment: Standard army officers waistbelt and cross strap.

Weapons: Air service officers undress dagger.

171. Norway: Chief Petty Officer (Kvartermester II. Kl.), England, 1941

The uniform is basically the same as that worn by officers, but with a simpler cap badge, and chevrons on the cuffs. The badge on the left sleeve is that of the gunnery branch.

Equipment: Standard army pattern leather equipment.

172. Poland: Seaman (Marynarz) O.R.P. (ship of the Polish Republic) Garland, Haifa, 1944

In addition to the Polish uniform illustrated ratings also received the British tropical uniform (78).

173. Poland: Sub Lieutenant (Podporucznik mar.) E. Liber, O.R.P. Krakoviak, England, 1942

This uniform was worn by officers, warrant officers, chief petty and petty officers.

Weapons: As officer of the watch he wears the M.1921 naval sword and belt.

174. Poland: Leading Seaman (Mat), England, 1941

The pre-war hat tally bore the inscription O.R.P. (ship of the Polish Republic) and the name of the ship, but at the beginning of the war a new pattern with *Marynarka Wojenna* was introduced. Gaiters or marching boots were worn by ratings on duty on land, and officers wore black leather gaiters.

Equipment: Army pattern ammunition pouches.

Weapons: Polish 7.9 mm. M.1929 service rifle.

175. Poland: Major H. M. Siess, commander Light Bomber Wing (Dyon) Hutniki, Poland, 1938

On the left sleeve of the flying suit Siess wears his badges of rank. In winter pilots wore brown leather flying clothing and equipment of French manufacture.

176. Poland: 2nd Lieutenant (Podporucznik) Stefan Lintzel, 22nd Squadron, 2nd Air Regiment, Hutniki, Poland, 1939

On the left breast pocket of his standard service dress (worn also by warrant officers and senior n.c.o.s) Lintzel wears the badges of the Air Force Officers School, above that of the Junior Military School for Boys.

Equipment: Officers waistbelt and cross strap.

Weapons: M.1924 dagger for air force and armoured corps officers. The naval pattern was identical but in gilt finish.

177. Poland: Flight Sergeant (Starzy Sierzant), eastern Poland, 1939
The working uniform was basically the same for all ranks, but the version for officers was of superior quality. Ground crew also wore the black beret with various types and colours of overalls.

178. Rumania: Captain (Capitänul), Russia, 1942
The side cap is that of the Luftwaffe with Rumanian badge. In addition to the shoulder straps, rank badges were also worn on the front of the side cap, and on the left breast of the flying suit. The badge on the left breast is that of a military pilot.

179. Rumania: Admiral (Amiral), Crimea, 1942
The standard service dress for officers and chief petty officers was very similar to the British pattern.

180. Slovakia: Captain (Kapitán), Bratislava 1942
This is basically the service dress of the old Czech army, but with an opened collared tunic. The military pilots badge is worn on the right breast.

181. U.S.A.: Midshipman 1st Class, U.S. Naval Academy, Annapolis, summer, 1941
This Brigade Chief Petty Officer wears the special cadet rank badges on the upper right sleeve, and narrow gold lace rings of a midshipman on his cuffs. This uniform is still in current use.

Weapons: U.S. .300 Enfield 1917 rifle and M.19 bayonet.

182. U.S.A.: Lieutenant Paul L. Joachim, America, November 1943
This officer wears the regulation greatcoat with rank distinction lace on the shoulder straps and in black on the cuffs. The newly introduced side or 'garrison' cap bore the U.S. Navy badge on the right, and rank badge on the left front.

183. U.S.A.: Captain, America, 1942
The blue service dress was worn by officers, warrant officers and chief petty officers, as well as by officers in the various auxiliary organisations such as the Coast Guard and Maritime Service.

184. U.S.A.: Petty Officer 3rd Class America, 1941
The rating badge on the right sleeve indicated that the sailor belonged to the seaman branch. The blue 'Donald Duck' hat was not popular because of its association with the Walt Disney character and so the white working hat was worn almost exclusively during the war.

185. U.S.A.: Shore Patrolman, London, England, July 1942
Here the white working hat, which showed up well in the black-out, is being worn with the peacoat, and canvas gaiters which were issued to ratings for wear on duty on land.

Equipment: Night stick, woven belt, and gas mask.

186. U.S.A.: Chief Petty Officer, America, 1941
The cap badge is the special pattern for C.P.O.s and the jacket was similar

to that worn by officers, except that it had eight instead of six buttons. C.P.O.s with less than twelve years' service were not entitled to gold chevrons. Each red stripe on the left cuff represented four years' service.

187. U.S.A.: Admiral William D. Leahy, Washington, 1943

As President Roosevelt's personal Chief of Staff, Leahy wears a gold lanyard on his light khaki service dress. The wearing of gold chin strap and peak embroidery was optional with all but full dress.

188. U.S.A.: Vice Admiral Halsey, Pearl Harbor, 1942

Halsey wearing white service uniform has just been awarded the Distinguished Service Medal. The white uniform for chief petty officers was open and worn with white shirt and black tie.

189. U.S.A.: Seaman, America, 1943

In summer ratings wore the white undress uniform with hat, which for cadets had a blue line around the top of the turn back.

Equipment: Standard army pattern woven ammunition belt.

Weapons: U.S. .300 Enfield 1917 rifle and M.1942 bayonet.

190. U.S.A.: Petty Officer 2nd Class, Atlantic Ocean, 1942

Rank badges were often painted in red for ratings and yellow for officers on the front of the anti-blast helmet. Foul weather clothing included the oilskin or 'slicker' suit and waterproof boots or 'arctics'.

Equipment: Woven waist belt and leather pistol holster.

191. U.S.A.: Seaman 2nd Class, Atlantic Ocean, 1943

The rating wears the M.1940 steel helmet with his division painted on the front, winter jacket and dungaree trousers.

192. U.S.A.: Seaman 1st Class South Pacific, 1945

The water-repellent 'jungle cloth' winter jacket is here worn with kapok life jacket and blue dungaree trousers, and 'arctics'. The helmet is the special 'Talker Mk. II' which was designed to be worn over headphones, by personnel on communications duty.

193. U.S.A.: Lieutenant Junior Grade Andrew Vanderwall, *U.S.S. Princeton*, Saipan, June 1944

Over the AN-S-31 (Army Navy Summer 31) flying suit, this Avenger pilot wears a 'life preserver vest', revolver suspended on the left breast from an ammunition belt, knife, and combat or 'escape' shoes.

194. U.S.A.: Captain W. F. Kline, U.S.N.

Kline wears the green working uniform for naval aviation personnel with black rank distinction lace on the cuffs. He is holding an ashtray given to him by members of the Fleet Air Arm.

195. U.S.A.: Flight Deck Officer, *U.S.S. Princeton*, Saipan, June 1944

Carriermen wore brightly coloured cloth helmets and shirts with their function or team number painted in large letters or numerals on the front and back.

196. U.S.A.: Corporal U.S. Marine Contingent, London, England, October 1942
On the left sleeve of his dress blue tunic he wears corporal's stripes and four year service stripe. The badges on the left breast are the sharpshooters badge and medal with dates of awards, expert rifleman's and pistol shot's bar suspended beneath it.

Equipment: Full dress white waist belt with brass plate and white bayonet sheath.

Weapons: U.S. .30 Caliber M1 rifle (Garand).

197. U.S.A.: Marine Harry Kiriziane in the ruins of Naha, Okinawa, May 1944
From March 1944 the typical Marine camouflage uniform began to be replaced by a new two-piece herringbone-twill (Olive Drab No. 7) combat uniform, with 'U.S.M.C.' and corps badge printed in black on the left breast pocket.

Equipment: Standard U.S. Army woven equipment.

Weapons: U.S. Caliber .30 M1 rifle (Garand).

198. U.S.A.: Captain U.S.M.C. Ship Detachment, Augusta, Georgia
The green service dress was basically identical in cut for all ranks, while officers uniforms were made of gabardine, and other ranks from serge. Ship detachments wore a red shoulder flash in the shape of a rhomboid

charged with a yellow sea horse superimposed on a blue anchor, on the left sleeve at shoulder height.

Equipment: Standard army pattern woven belt with pouch for pistol ammunition clips, and brown leather holster. There were two patterns of waist belt; the belt illustrated had eyelets from which the various items of equipment were suspended, while the belt issued for wear with full equipment did not have the eyelets, since these appeared on the woven ammunition pouches.

199. U.S.A.: Marine, New Britain, February 1943
The fatigue cap with Marine emblem in black on the front is here worn with camouflage jacket, herringbone twill trousers and waterproof boots.

Equipment: Woven waistbelt, ammunition clip pouch and holster.

Weapons: U.S. .45 M.1928 Thompson A1 sub machine gun.

200. U.S.A.: Petty Officer 3rd Class Samoan Fita Fita Guard
Members of this all-native unit were assigned to guard American Samoa, wore national dress in the same basic colour schemes as the U.S. Navy. Illustrated here is the white dress uniform with rating badge on the front of the *Lava-Lava*. Other orders of dress incorporated a khaki drill turban and *Lava-Lava*, or red turban and blue *Lava-Lava*.

Equipment: Standard U.S. Army woven belt and ammunition pouches.

Weapons: U.S. .30 Caliber Model 1903 rifle and M.1905 bayonet.

201. U.S.A.: Major Theodor Olsen, executive officer 'Lilly Packin Death Falcons' Squadron, 1 Marine Air Wing, Leyte Gulf, October 1944
Olsen wears the AN-S-31 summer flying suit, life jacket and escape shoes. Pilots flying over jungle regions in the Far East were also equipped with the Type C-1 Emergency Sustenance Vest – an adjustable vest-like garment fitted with pockets into which items of survival kit (anything from lavatory paper to fish-sewing kit in plastic container) were conveniently stowed. It was worn under the life jacket and parachute.

202. U.S.A.: Captain Clark Gable, 8th U.S. Army Air Force, England, 1941
Gable wears the typical crushed cap affected by aircrew, and raincoat with rank badges on the shoulder straps.

203. U.S.A.: Lieutenant General Lewis M. Brereton, commanding general 9th Air Force, England, April 1943
The 'Ike' blouse with diagonal slash pockets was the forerunner of the M.1944 khaki service uniform which became general issue in 1945. On his right breast he wears the Army Distinguished Unit Badge.

204. U.S.A.: Corporal (5th Grade) 9th Air Force, England, April 1943
M.P.s wore army service dress adorned with white cap cover (which sometimes covered the whole cap), white pistol lanyard, gloves, and leggings, and a whistle on a chain on the left breast.

205. U.S.A.: Staff Sergeant D. A. Mayo, England, 1944
Mayo wears a two-piece shearling flying suit with type AN (army navy) -H (heated) 16 helmet, A-6 boots and life preserving vest.

206. U.S.A.: 1st Lieutenant James G. Stevenson, England, 1943
The A(army) 2 flying jacket was one of the most popular garments and was worn both on and off duty. The beige trousers were known as 'pinks'.

207. U.S.A.: Private Joe Arritola, 9th Air Force, England, 1944
Joe wears the fatigue 'baseball' cap and working overalls on which rank badges were often drawn with indelible pencil.

208. U.S.A.: Navigator, England, 1944
This outfit includes the Type A (army) helmet with A-14 demand oxygen mask, B-15 jacket, A-11 trousers, A-6 boots and A-11 gloves. In his hand he carries a computer.

209. U.S.A.: Gunner, England, 1944
Beginning in 1943 crews of heavy bombers began to be equipped with protective armour against shrapnel, and the first suits were produced by the famous British swordsmiths Wilkinsons, but these were later superseded by the American pattern illustrated. A helmet designed to fit over the earphones was also introduced.

210. U.S.A.: Waist gunner B-17 bomber, England, 1944
The Type AN-H-16 helmet is here

worn with the F-2 electrically heated suit, and special boots.

Weapons: .50 caliber M-2 machine gun.

211. U.S.S.R.: Senior Lieutenant (Starshy Leytenant), Soviet Naval Mission, England, 1943

This officer wears the standard service dress with rank distinction lace on the cuffs, in addition to the shoulder straps, which indicated that he was a line or executive officer.

212. U.S.S.R.: Captain of the Third Rank (Kapitan tret 'yevo ranga), Soviet Naval Mission, England, November, 1941

Prior to the re-introduction of shoulder boards in January 1943 there was no distinction between executive and other officers, since all wore rank distinction lace on the cuffs.

213. U.S.S.R.: Petty Officer 1st Class (Starshina pervoy stati), May Day Parade, Moscow, 1940

Petty officers with more than five years' service were entitled to wear the peaked cap with 'square rig'. The boatswain's whistle was worn on duty and with parade dress by the front rank and the file nearest the saluting base.

Weapons: Soviet Moisin Nagant 7.62 mm. M.1931/30 rifle and bayonet.

214. U.S.S.R.: Seaman (Krasnoflotets), England, December 1943

This member of the ship's choir wears the white summer uniform (No. 1), which was worn between 1 May and 1 October. Ships or establishments could receive, in recognition of exceptional conduct, the designation 'guards'. This entitled sailors to wear the orange and black ribbon (248) on their hats, and officers and warrant officers the guards badge on the right breast.

215. U.S.S.R.: Captain Lieutenant (Kapitan Leytenant) Fissanovitch, Baltic Sea, 1944

As a submarine commander he wears a fur *ushanka* which had a leather top, while the other ranks version was cloth. The coat and sea boots were part of the vessel's stock of protective clothing.

216. U.S.S.R.: Seaman (Krasnoflotets), Black Sea, 1941

On the left breast of the working jumper ratings wore a series of three numbers which indicated their branch (2 gunnery), station, and duty or crew number. The steel helmet was the standard army M.1936 or 1940 pattern painted light blue.

Equipment: Gas mask slung over right shoulder.

217. U.S.S.R.: Leading Seaman (Starshy Krasnoflotets), Marine Detachment, Sevastopol, summer 1943

During the siege, and while participating in other land battles naval personnel wore army uniform, but in order to preserve their naval identity striped vests and sailors' hats were proudly retained.

218. U.S.S.R.: Rear Admiral (Kontr Admiral) Vaenga, Murmansk, 1941

This admiral was in charge of a Soviet Naval Aviation unit co-operating with the British Fighter Wing stationed in his command. He wears an unofficial leather greatcoat, breeches and boots.

219. U.S.S.R.: Seaman (Krasnoflotets), Marine Detachment, Black Sea, 1943
Marines were identified by a foul anchor worn on the upper left sleeve. The medal is for the defence of Sevastopol which was instituted on 22 December 1942.

Weapons: Soviet 7.62 mm. PPSH sub machine gun 1941, stick grenade M.1914/30, and ammunition belts.

220. U.S.S.R.: Captain (Kapitan) B. Diky, Soviet Air Force Mission, England, November 1942
This shows the 1935 pattern blue service dress for regular air force personnel. An other ranks version of this uniform was also worn by the Air Force Guard of Honour for visiting dignitaries.

221. U.S.S.R.: Senior Sergeant (Starshy Sergant) N. Kilimenro, Russia, 1942
On his collar patches a senior sergeant would have worn three red enamel triangles. As a Tomahawk pilot Kilimenro wears the standard summer flying suit and blue *pilotka*.

222. U.S.S.R.: Major, Vaenga near Murmansk, autumn 1941
This liaison officer with the R.A.F. wing serving in northern Russia wears a typical pre-war leather flying coat, and blue peaked cap or *furashka*.

223. U.S.S.R.: Hero of the Soviet Union Lieutenant (Leytenant), Kankeshev Ahmet Haptal, Russia, 1943
This Caucasian fighter ace wears the newly introduced shirt, in traditional cut, with stand collar and shoulder boards. In common with fighter pilots of most nations summer flying dress usually consisted of everyday uniform with parachute and flying helmet.

224. U.S.S.R.: Senior Lieutenant (Starshy Leytenant), parachute troops, Russia, 1942
In action parachutists wore a grey overall and cloth helmet, until the introduction, later in the war, of a camouflage uniform. Qualified parachutists wore a small enamelled badge above the left breast pocket. This officer wears the Order of the Red Banner which was originally instituted on 16 September 1918. From 19 June 1943 it was to be worn suspended from a red ribbon.

225. U.S.S.R.: Bomber pilot, Leningrad front, winter, 1941–42
Winter flying clothing was not electrically heated but relied on fur lining to helmet, overall, and gauntlets to keep the wearer warm.

226. Croatia: Seaman (Mornar), Dubrovnik, 1942
This is the uniform of the Yugoslav navy with the addition of a German-pattern hat and Croatian cap badge. The hat tally remained unchanged.

Equipment: Yugoslav infantry pattern leather equipment.

Weapons: French Gras 11 mm. single shot rifle.

227. Yugoslavia: Senior Lieutenant Commander (Nadporučnik bojnog broda), Lepetic, England, 28 October 1943
Lepetic wears British uniform with Yugoslav cap badge. Ratings also received Royal Navy clothing and hat tally with *Ratna Mornarica* in yellow block letters.

228. Croatia: Lieutenant Commander (Poručnik bojnog broda), Dubrovnik, 1942
This officer wears Yugoslav uniform, which resembled that of the Italian navy. The *passants* were later replaced by German-pattern shoulder straps in the 1944 regulations.

229. Yugoslavia: Captain (Kapitan) No. 352 Squadron R.A.F., Canne, Italy, September 1944
This flight commander wears British tropical clothing with Yugoslav side cap, and R.A.F. rank badges (flight lieutenant) on the shoulder straps, and Yugoslav National Liberation ones on the left breast.

230. Yugoslavia: Captain (Kapetan bojnog broda), Egypt, May 1941
This officer was one of a group of Yugoslav Air Force officers who flew a Dornier 17 to Egypt to join the Allies. He wears regulation uniform with rank badges on the cuffs and shoulder straps, and military pilots badge on the right breast.

231. Croatia: Lieutenant (Poručnik) Agram, summer 1942

This officer was a member of the first full regiment of the Croatian Air Force to leave for service on the eastern front. He wears Yugoslav uniform with rank badges on the cuffs and shoulder straps. The badge above the German national emblem on the right breast is the transitional model of Croatian military pilots wings.

Swords
232. German naval officers sword
233. British Royal Navy officers sword
234. Italian Royal Naval officers sword M.1861
235. Imperial Japanese Naval officers sword
236. United States Naval officers sword

Daggers
237. Croatian Air Force officers dagger
238. French Air Force officers dagger. The model for senior n.c.o.s and warrant officers had a blue grip
239. German Air Force dagger, M.1937
240. Royal Hungarian Air Force officers dagger
241. Polish Air Force officers dagger. Originally introduced on 7 October 1924 for Air Force and armoured corps officers in gilt finish, but on the 25 September 1937 it was changed to silver fittings so that naval officers could have it in gilt
242. Slovak Air Force officers dagger

Collars

BIBLIOGRAPHY

AAF (*The official guide to the Army Air Forces*) Pocket Books Inc., New York 1944

ABC of the RAF edited by Sir John Hammerton, new and enlarged edition, London 1942

Allies in Arms edited by Owen Rutter, Lincolns-Prager Publishers Ltd, London 1941

ROGER JAMES BENDER *Air Organisations of the Third Reich, The Luftwaffe*, R. James Bender Publishing, California 1972

KOMMANDØRKAPTAJN E. BORG *Den Danske Marines Uniformer Gennemtre Århundreder*, Strubes Forlag, Viborg 1974

COMMANDANT E. L. BUCQUOY *Les Uniformes de l'Armée Française* (*Terre-Mer-Air*), illustrated by M. Toussaint, Les Editions Militaires Illustrées, Paris 1935

J. A. CARTER *Allied Bayonets of World War 2*, Arms and Armour Press, London 1969

JERZY B. CYNK *History of the Polish Air Force 1918–1968*, Osprey Publishing Ltd, Reading 1972

Dress Regulations for Officers of the Royal Air Force (Air Ministry Publication 1358), 2nd (abridged) edition, H.M.S.O., 1939

GILBERT GROSVENOR et al. *Insignia and Decorations of the U.S. Armed Forces*, revised edition 1 Dec. 1944, National Geographic Society, Washington D.C. 1945

ELIO and VITTORIO DEL GUIDICE *Uniformi Militari Italiane dal 1861 ai Giorni Nostri*, Vol. II dal 1934 oggi, Bramante Editrice, Milan 1964

O. V. HARINTONOV *Uniforms and Marks of Distinction* (*Insignia*) *of the Soviet Army 1911–1958*, Artillery Historical Museum, Leningrad 1958

EBERHARD HETTLER *Uniformen der Deutschen Wehrmacht – Heer, Kriegsmarine und Luftwaffe*, Uniformen-Markt Verlag, Berlin 1939; Nachtrag (supplement) 1939–40, Uniformen-Markt Verlag, Berlin 1940

Intendance Marine *Uniformes et Marques Distinctives des Militaires non-Officiers de l'Armée de Mer L'Imprimérie Jemnapes*, Paris 1938

Identification (*The World's Military, Naval and Air Uniforms, Insignia and Flags*), Military Service Publishing Company, Harrisburg, Penn., 1943

BERTIL JACOBSEN *Sjömansuniformen i olika Marina Genom Tiderna*, Orlogspostens Förlag, Stockholm 1946

Jane's Fighting Ships 1944–45 edited by Francis E. McMurtrie, Sampson Low, Marston, 1944

KNÖTEL/JANTKE/SIEG *Die Soldaten Europas Series 1* (loose plates), Czechoslovakia I, Poland I, England I, Austria I, Italy I, and France I, Series 2, Russia I, II, Belgium I, Czechoslovakia II, Poland II, and France II, Militärverlag Karl Siegismund, Berlin 1937–39.

HERBERT KNÖTEL JNR and HERBERT SIEG *Handbuch der Uniformkunde* (3rd edn), Stand vom Jahre 1937, Helmut Gerhard Schulz, Hamburg 1937 (reprinted 1956)

L'Armée de l'Air Tenues de Campagne Métropole et Colonies 1945 (No. 2), Les Éditions Militaires Illustrées, Paris 1945

J. P. MALLMAN SHOWELL *U-boats under the Swastika*, Ian Allen Ltd, Shepperton, 1973

BERNARD LE MAREC *Les Françaises Libres et leurs Emblèmes*, Charles Lavauzelle & Cie, 1964

COMMANDER W. E. MAY, W. Y. CARMAN and J. TANNER *Badges and Insignia of the British Armed Services*, Adam and Charles Black, London 1974

Ministero della Forze Armata *Isttruzione Provvisoria sull'Uniforme dell 'Esercito Nazionale Repubblicano*, 1 September 1944

ANDREW MOLLO *Army Uniforms of World War 2*, Blandford Press Ltd, London 1973

TADAO NAKATA *Imperial Japanese Uniforms and Equipments*, Sankei Publishing Company, Tokyo 1973. Japanese edition with English language supplement, Arms and Armour Press, London 1975

COLONEL ROBERT H. RANKIN USMAC *Uniforms of the Sea Services*, United States Naval Institute, Annapolis 1962

GUIDO ROSIGNOLI *Army Badges and Insignia of World War 2: Great Britain Poland, Belgium, Italy, U.S.S.R., U.S.A., and Germany*, Blandford Press, London 1972

GUIDO ROSIGNOLI *Army Badges and Insignia of World War 2 (Book 2): British Commonwealth, China, Czechoslovakia, Denmark, Finland, France, Japan, The Netherlands, Yugoslavia*, Blandford Press, London 1975

J. E. and W. H. B. SMITH *Small Arms of the World (a basic manual of military small arms)*, 9th edn, Stackpole Books, Harrisburg, Pennsylvania 1969

There's Freedom in the Air (the official story of the Allied air forces from occupied countries), London, H.M.S.O. 1944

JAMES C. TILY *The Uniforms of the United States Navy*, Thomas Yoseloff, New York 1964

Uniform Regulations for officers of the Fleet (Admiralty Publication BR 81) 1937, reprinted 1941

Uniformele Armatei Romane 1830–1930, Muzeul Militar National, Bucaresti 1930

Uniforms Decorations Medals and Badges of the U.S. Navy, taken from the Navy Uniform Regulations 1941, U.S. Government Printing Office, Washington 1941

Uniforms and Insignia, A Joint U.S. Army and Navy Publication (J.A.N.I.), Brazil (Nov. 43), France (Jul. 43), German Navy (Jul. 44), German Air Force (Aug. & Nov. 43), Greece (Feb. 45), Italian Navy (Sept. 43), Italian Air Force (Oct. 43), Japanese Navy (Sept. 43), Netherlands Navy (Oct. 43), Portuguese Navy (June 43), Spain (Mar. 43), and Sweden. Prepared by the Military Inteligence Service and Division of Naval Intelligence, U.S.A.

J. ZIENERT *Unsere Marineuniform*, Verlag Helmut Gerhard Schulz, Hamburg 1970

INDEX TO ILLUSTRATIONS